Workshop on Computationally Hard Problems and Joint Inference in Speech and Language Processing 2006

Held at HLT/NAACL 2006

New York, New York, USA
9 June 2006

ISBN: 978-1-61738-494-3

Printed from e-media with permission by:

Curran Associates, Inc.
57 Morehouse Lane
Red Hook, NY 12571
www.proceedings.com

Some format issues inherent in the e-media version may also appear in this print version.

Printed by Curran Associates, Inc. (2010)

Association for Computational Linguistics
209 N. Eighth Street
Stroudsburg, Pennsylvania 18360

Phone: 1-570-476-8006
Fax: 1-570-476-0860

acl@aclweb.org

Introduction

We are pleased to present the proceedings of the Workshop on Computationally Hard Problems and Joint Inference in Speech and Language Processing, held at HLT/NAACL 2006 in New York City, New York.

Recent work on ranking, sampling and other approximate solutions to natural language processing problems indicate that researchers are coming back to the hard problems in speech and text, for which efficient algorithms are not known to exist. In addition, there has been increasing interest in moving away from systems that make chains of local decisions independently, and instead toward systems that make multiple decisions jointly using global information. The goal of this workshop is to bring together researchers working on NLP problems whose solutions are computationally hard—whether because the problem is not well modeled by only local features, or because the problem is best solved in a joint, rather than pipelined, manner.

We are grateful to the program committee for providing thoughtful and helpful reviews of the submitted papers. We also thank our invited speakers, Jeff Bilmes, Chris Manning, Dan Roth, and Giorgio Satta. Finally, we thank the organizers of the main HLT/NAACL 2006 conference, without which this workshop would not be possible.

Ryan McDonald, Charles Sutton, Hal Daumé III, Andrew McCallum, Jeff Bilmes, and Fernando Pereira
organizers

Invited Speakers:

Jeff Bilmes, University of Washington
Chris Manning, Stanford University
Dan Roth, University of Illinois
Giorgio Satta, University of Padua

Organizers:

Ryan McDonald, University of Pennsylvania
Charles Sutton, University of Massachusetts
Hal Daumé III, Information Sciences Institute, University of Southern California
Andrew McCallum, University of Massachusetts
Fernando Pereira, University of Pennsylvania
Jeff Bilmes, University of Washington

Program Committee:

Razvan Bunescu, University of Texas
Bill Byrne, University of Cambridge
Xavier Carreras, Technical University of Catalonia
Ozgur Cetin, University of California, Berekely
David Chiang, Information Sciences Institute, University of Southern California
Michael Collins, Massachusetts Institute of Technology
Jason Eisner, Johns Hopkins University
Radu Florian, IBM TJ Watson Research Center
Eric Fosler-Lussier, The Ohio State University
Dan Gildea, University of Rochester
Ralph Grishman, NYU
Julia Hockenmaier, University of Pennsylvania
Eric Horvitz, Microsoft
Liang Huang, University of Pennsylvania
Thorsten Joachims, Cornell University
Katrin Kirchhoff, University of Washington
Philipp Koehn, University of Edinburgh
Shankar Kumar, Google
Chris Manning, Stanford University
Lluís Màrquez, Technical University of Catalonia
Gideon Mann, University of Massachusetts
Erik McDermott, NTT
Ray Mooney, University of Texas
Franz Och, Google

Kishore Papineni, IBM TJ Watson Research Center
Chris Quirk, Microsoft
Brian Roark, Oregon Graduate Institute
Dan Roth, University of Illinois
Salim Roukos, IBM TJ Watson Research Center
Libin Shen, University of Pennsylvania
Koichi Shinoda, Tokyo Institute of Technology
Noah Smith, Johns Hopkins University
Andreas Stolcke, SRI
Ben Taskar, University of California, Berkeley

Table of Contents

A Syntax-Directed Translator with Extended Domain of Locality
Liang Huang, Kevin Knight and Aravind Joshi 1

Efficient Dynamic Programming Search Algorithms for Phrase-Based SMT
Christoph Tillmann 9

Computational Challenges in Parsing by Classification
Joseph Turian and I. Dan Melamed 17

All-word Prediction as the Ultimate Confusible Disambiguation
Antal van den Bosch 25

A Probabilistic Search for the Best Solution Among Partially Completed Candidates
Filip Ginter, Aleksandr Mylläri and Tapio Salakoski 33

Practical Markov Logic Containing First-Order Quantifiers with Application to Identity Uncertainty
Aron Culotta and Andrew McCallum 41

Re-Ranking Algorithms for Name Tagging
Heng Ji, Cynthia Rudin and Ralph Grishman 49

Conference Program

Friday, June 9, 2006

8:45–9:00 Opening Remarks

9:00–9:40 Invited Talk by Giorgio Satta

9:40–10:05 *A Syntax-Directed Translator with Extended Domain of Locality*
Liang Huang, Kevin Knight and Aravind Joshi

10:05–10:30 *Efficient Dynamic Programming Search Algorithms for Phrase-Based SMT*
Christoph Tillmann

10:30–11:00 Break

11:00–11:25 *Computational Challenges in Parsing by Classification*
Joseph Turian and I. Dan Melamed

11:25–11:50 *All-word Prediction as the Ultimate Confusible Disambiguation*
Antal van den Bosch

11:50–12:30 Invited Talk by Jeff Bilmes

12:30–14:00 Lunch

14:00–14:25 *A Probabilistic Search for the Best Solution Among Partially Completed Candidates*
Filip Ginter, Aleksandr Mylläri and Tapio Salakoski

14:25–14:50 *Practical Markov Logic Containing First-Order Quantifiers with Application to Identity Uncertainty*
Aron Culotta and Andrew McCallum

14:50–15:30 Invited Talk by Chris Manning

15:30–16:00 Break

16:00–16:25 *Re-Ranking Algorithms for Name Tagging*
Heng Ji, Cynthia Rudin and Ralph Grishman

Friday, June 9, 2006 (continued)

16:25–17:05 Invited Talk by Dan Roth

A Syntax-Directed Translator with Extended Domain of Locality

Liang Huang
Dept. of Comp. & Info. Sci.
Univ. of Pennsylvania
Philadelphia, PA 19104
lhuang3@cis.upenn.edu

Kevin Knight
Info. Sci. Inst.
Univ. of Southern California
Marina del Rey, CA 90292
knight@isi.edu

Aravind Joshi
Dept. of Comp. & Info. Sci.
Univ. of Pennsylvania
Philadelphia, PA 19104
joshi@linc.cis.upenn.edu

Abstract

A syntax-directed translator first parses the source-language input into a parse-tree, and then recursively converts the tree into a string in the target-language. We model this conversion by an extended tree-to-string transducer that have multi-level trees on the source-side, which gives our system more expressive power and flexibility. We also define a direct probability model and use a linear-time dynamic programming algorithm to search for the best derivation. The model is then extended to the general log-linear framework in order to rescore with other features like n-gram language models. We devise a simple-yet-effective algorithm to generate non-duplicate k-best translations for n-gram rescoring. Initial experimental results on English-to-Chinese translation are presented.

1 Introduction

The concept of *syntax-directed (SD) translation* was originally proposed in compiling (Irons, 1961; Lewis and Stearns, 1968), where the source program is parsed into a tree representation that guides the generation of the object code. Following Aho and Ullman (1972), a *translation*, as a set of string pairs, can be specified by a *syntax-directed translation schema* (SDTS), which is essentially a synchronous context-free grammar (SCFG) that generates two languages simultaneously. An SDTS also induces a *translator*, a device that performs the transformation from input string to output string. In this context, an SD translator consists of two components, a source-language parser and a recursive converter which is usually modeled as a top-down tree-to-string transducer (Gécseg and Steinby, 1984). The relationship among these concepts is illustrated in Fig. 1.

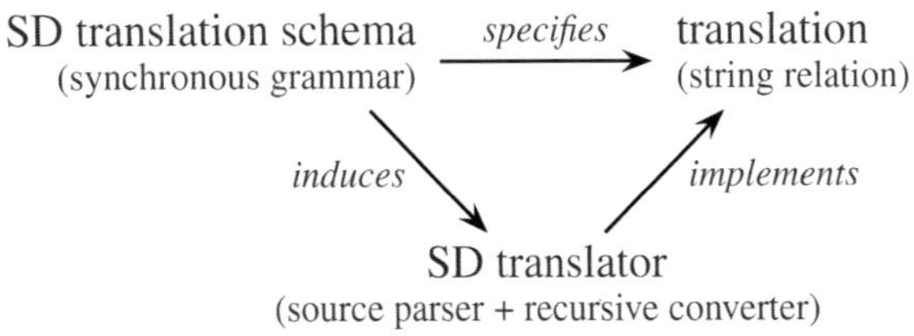

Figure 1: The relationship among SD concepts, adapted from (Aho and Ullman, 1972).

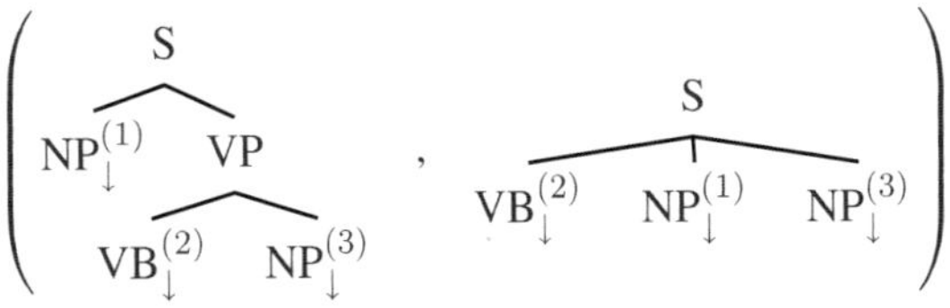

Figure 2: An example of complex reordering represented as an STSG rule, which is beyond any SCFG.

This paper adapts the idea of syntax-directed translator to statistical machine translation (MT). We apply stochastic operations at each node of the source-language parse-tree and search for the best derivation (a sequence of translation steps) that converts the whole tree into some target-language string with the highest probability. However, the structural divergence across languages often results in non-isomorphic parse-trees that is beyond the power of SCFGs. For example, the *S(VO)* structure in English is translated into a *VSO* word-order in Arabic, an instance of *complex reordering* not captured by any

Workshop on Computationally Hard Problemsand Joint Inference in Speech and Language Processing, pages 1–8,
New York City, New York, June 2006. ©2006 Association for Computational Linguistics

SCFG (Fig. 2).

To alleviate the non-isomorphism problem, (synchronous) grammars with richer expressive power have been proposed whose rules apply to larger fragments of the tree. For example, Shieber and Schabes (1990) introduce synchronous tree-adjoining grammar (STAG) and Eisner (2003) uses a synchronous tree-substitution grammar (STSG), which is a restricted version of STAG with no adjunctions. STSGs and STAGs generate more *tree relations* than SCFGs, e.g. the non-isomorphic tree pair in Fig. 2. This extra expressive power lies in the *extended domain of locality* (EDL) (Joshi and Schabes, 1997), i.e., elementary structures beyond the scope of one-level context-free productions. Besides being linguistically motivated, the need for EDL is also supported by empirical findings in MT that one-level rules are often inadequate (Fox, 2002; Galley et al., 2004). Similarly, in the tree-transducer terminology, Graehl and Knight (2004) define extended tree transducers that have multi-level trees on the source-side.

Since an SD translator separates the source-language analysis from the recursive transformation, the domains of locality in these two modules are orthogonal to each other: in this work, we use a CFG-based Treebank parser but focuses on the extended domain in the recursive converter. Following Galley et al. (2004), we use a special class of *extended tree-to-string transducer* (**xRs** for short) with multi-level left-hand-side (LHS) trees.[1] Since the right-hand-side (RHS) string can be viewed as a flat one-level tree with the same nonterminal root from LHS (Fig. 2), this framework is closely related to STSGs: they both have extended domain of locality on the source-side, while our framework remains as a CFG on the target-side. For instance, an equivalent **xRs** rule for the complex reordering in Fig. 2 would be

$$\text{S}(x_1\text{:NP, VP}(x_2\text{:VB}, x_3\text{:NP})) \rightarrow x_2\ x_1\ x_3$$

While Section 3 will define the model formally, we first proceed with an example translation from English to Chinese (note in particular that the inverted phrases between source and target):

[1]Throughout this paper, we will use LHS and source-side interchangeably (so are RHS and target-side). In accordance with our experiments, we also use English and Chinese as the source and target languages, opposite to the Foreign-to-English convention of Brown et al. (1993).

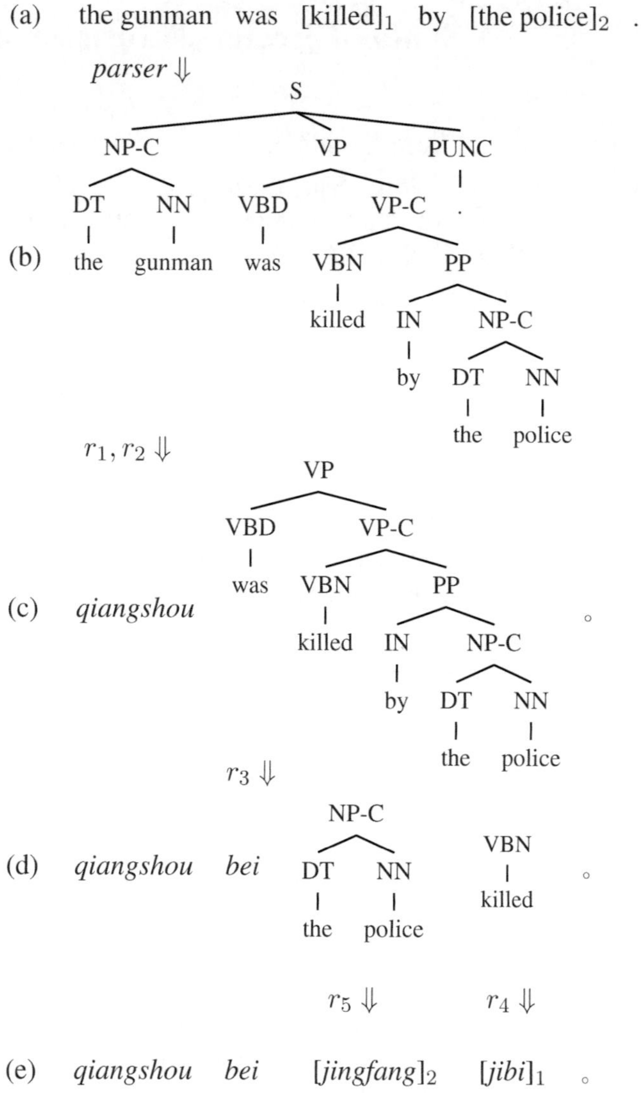

Figure 3: A synatx-directed translation process for Example (1).

(1) the gunman was killed by the police .

qiangshou bei *jingfang jibi* 。
[gunman] [passive] [police] [killed] .

Figure 3 shows how the translator works. The English sentence (a) is first parsed into the tree in (b), which is then recursively converted into the Chinese string in (e) through five steps. First, at the root node, we apply the rule r_1 which preserves the top-level word-order and translates the English period into its Chinese counterpart:

$$(r_1)\ \text{S}\ (x_1\text{:NP-C}\ x_2\text{:VP PUNC (.)}\ ) \rightarrow x_1\ x_2\ 。$$

Then, the rule r_2 grabs the whole sub-tree for "the gunman" and translates it as a phrase:

(r_2) NP-C (DT (the) NN (gunman)) $\rightarrow$ *qiangshou*

Now we get a "partial Chinese, partial English" sentence "*qiangshou* VP 。" as shown in Fig. 3 (c). Our recursion goes on to translate the VP sub-tree. Here we use the rule r_3 for the passive construction:

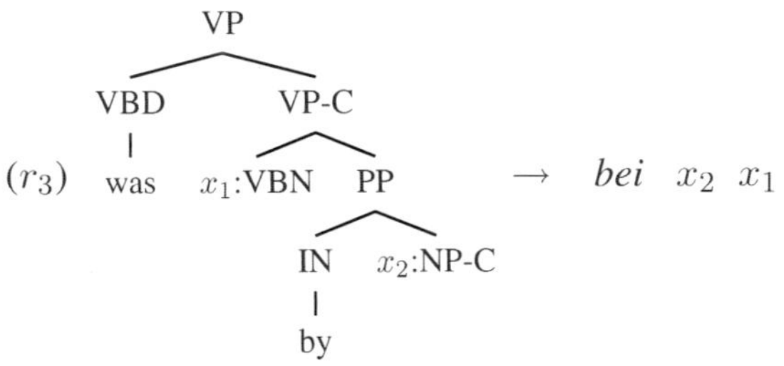

which captures the fact that the agent (NP-C, "the police") and the verb (VBN, "killed") are always inverted between English and Chinese in a passive voice. Finally, we apply rules r_4 and r_5 which perform phrasal translations for the two remaining subtrees in (d), respectively, and get the completed Chinese string in (e).

2 Previous Work

It is helpful to compare this approach with recent efforts in statistical MT. Phrase-based models (Koehn et al., 2003; Och and Ney, 2004) are good at learning local translations that are pairs of (consecutive) sub-strings, but often insufficient in modeling the reorderings of phrases themselves, especially between language pairs with very different word-order. This is because the generative capacity of these models lies within the realm of finite-state machinery (Kumar and Byrne, 2003), which is unable to process nested structures and long-distance dependencies in natural languages.

Syntax-based models aim to alleviate this problem by exploiting the power of synchronous rewriting systems. Both Yamada and Knight (2001) and Chiang (2005) use SCFGs as the underlying model, so their translation schemata are syntax-directed as in Fig. 1, but their translators are *not*: both systems do parsing and transformation in a joint search, essentially over a packed forest of parse-trees. To this end, their translators are not *directed* by a syntactic tree. Although their method potentially considers more than one single parse-tree as in our case, the packed representation of the forest restricts the scope of each transfer step to a one-level context-free rule, while our approach decouples the source-language analyzer and the recursive converter, so that the latter can have an extended domain of locality. In addition, our translator also enjoys a speed-up by this decoupling, with each of the two stages having a smaller search space. In fact, the recursive transfer step can be done by a a *linear-time* algorithm (see Section 5), and the parsing step is also fast with the modern Treebank parsers, for instance (Collins, 1999; Charniak, 2000). In contrast, their decodings are reported to be computationally expensive and Chiang (2005) uses aggressive pruning to make it tractable. There also exists a compromise between these two approaches, which uses a k-best list of parse trees (for a relatively small k) to approximate the full forest (see future work).

Besides, our model, as being linguistically motivated, is also more expressive than the formally syntax-based models of Chiang (2005) and Wu (1997). Consider, again, the passive example in rule r_3. In Chiang's SCFG, there is only one nonterminal X, so a corresponding rule would be

$$\langle \text{ was } X^{(1)} \text{ by } X^{(2)},\ \textit{bei}\ X^{(2)}\ X^{(1)} \rangle$$

which can also pattern-match the English sentence:

I was $[\text{asleep}]_1$ by $[\text{sunset}]_2$.

and translate it into Chinese as a passive voice. This produces very odd Chinese translation, because here "was A by B" in the English sentence is *not* a passive construction. By contrast, our model applies rule r_3 only if A is a past participle (VBN) and B is a noun phrase (NP-C). This example also shows that, one-level SCFG rule, even if informed by the Treebank as in (Yamada and Knight, 2001), is not enough to capture a common construction like this which is five levels deep (from VP to "by").

There are also some variations of syntax-directed translators where dependency structures are used in place of constituent trees (Lin, 2004; Ding and Palmer, 2005; Quirk et al., 2005). Although they share with this work the basic motivations and similar speed-up, it is difficult to specify re-ordering information within dependency elementary structures, so they either resort to heuristics (Lin) or a separate ordering model for linearization (the other two works).[2] Our approach, in contrast, explicitly models the re-ordering of sub-trees within individual transfer rules.

3 Extended Tree-to-String Tranducers

In this section, we define the formal machinery of our recursive transformation model as a special case of **xRs** transducers (Graehl and Knight, 2004) that has only one state, and each rule is linear (L) and non-deleting (N) with regarding to variables in the source and target sides (henth the name 1-**xRLNs**).

Definition 1. A **1-xRLNs transducer** is a tuple $(N, \Sigma, \Delta, \mathcal{R})$ where N is the set of nonterminals, Σ is the input alphabet, Δ is the output alphabet, and $\mathcal{R}$ is a set of rules. A rule in $\mathcal{R}$ is a tuple (t, s, ϕ) where:

1. t is the LHS tree, whose internal nodes are labeled by nonterminal symbols, and whose frontier nodes are labeled terminals from Σ or variables from a set $\mathcal{X} = \{x_1, x_2, \ldots\}$;
2. $s \in (\mathcal{X} \cup \Delta)^*$ is the RHS string;
3. ϕ is a mapping from $\mathcal{X}$ to nonterminals N.

We require each variable $x_i \in \mathcal{X}$ occurs *exactly once* in t and *exactly once* in s (linear and non-deleting).

We denote $\rho(t)$ to be the **root symbol** of tree t. When writing these rules, we avoid notational overhead by introducing a short-hand form from Galley et al. (2004) that integrates the mapping into the tree, which is used throughout Section 1. Following TSG terminology (see Figure 2), we call these "variable nodes" such as x_2:NP-C *substitution nodes*, since when applying a rule to a tree, these nodes will be matched with a sub-tree with the same root symbol.

We also define $|\mathcal{X}|$ to be the **rank** of the rule, i.e., the number of variables in it. For example, rules r_1 and r_3 in Section 1 are both of rank 2. If a rule has no variable, i.e., it is of rank zero, then it is called a *purely lexical rule*, which performs a phrasal translation as in phrase-based models. Rule r_2, for instance, can be thought of as a phrase pair $\langle$the gunman, *qiangshou*$\rangle$.

Informally speaking, a derivation in a transducer is a sequence of steps converting a source-language tree into a target-language string, with each step applying one tranduction rule. However, it can also be formalized as a tree, following the notion of *derivation-tree* in TAG (Joshi and Schabes, 1997):

[2]Although hybrid approaches, such as dependency grammars augmented with phrase-structure information (Alshawi et al., 2000), can do re-ordering easily.

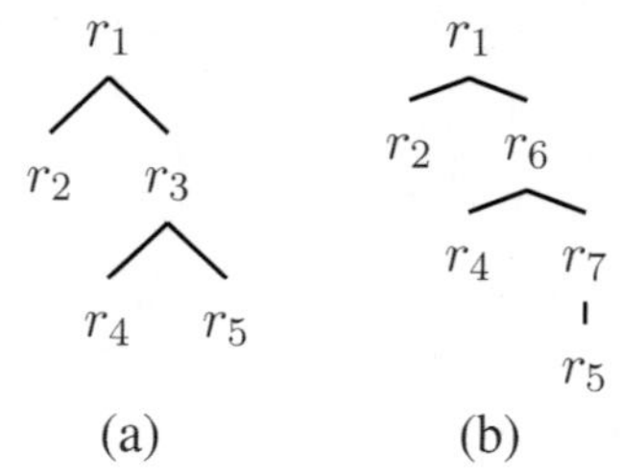

Figure 4: (a) the derivation in Figure 3; (b) another derviation producing the same output by replacing r_3 with r_6 and r_7, which provides another way of translating the passive construction:

(r_6) VP (VBD (was) VP-C (x_1:VBN x_2:PP)) $\rightarrow x_2\ x_1$

(r_7) PP (IN (by) x_1:NP-C) $\rightarrow$ *bei* x_1

Definition 2. A **derivation** d, its **source and target projections**, noted $\mathcal{E}(d)$ and $\mathcal{C}(d)$ respectively, are recursively defined as follows:

1. If $r = (t, s, \phi)$ is a purely lexical rule ($\phi = \emptyset$), then $d = r$ is a derivation, where $\mathcal{E}(d) = t$ and $\mathcal{C}(d) = s$;
2. If $r = (t, s, \phi)$ is a rule, and d_i is a (sub-)derivation with the root symbol of its source projection matches the corresponding substitution node in r, i.e., $\rho(\mathcal{E}(d_i)) = \phi(x_i)$, then $d = r(d_1, \ldots, d_m)$ is also a derivation, where $\mathcal{E}(d) = [x_i \mapsto \mathcal{E}(d_i)]t$ and $\mathcal{C}(d) = [x_i \mapsto \mathcal{C}(d_i)]s$.

Note that we use a short-hand notation $[x_i \mapsto y_i]t$ to denote the result of substituting each x_i with y_i in t, where x_i ranges over all variables in t.

For example, Figure 4 shows two derivations for the sentence pair in Example (1). In both cases, the source projection is the English tree in Figure 3 (b), and the target projection is the Chinese translation.

Galley et al. (2004) presents a linear-time algorithm for automatic extraction of these **xRs** rules from a parallel corpora with word-alignment and parse-trees on the source-side, which will be used in our experiments in Section 6.

4 Probability Models

4.1 Direct Model

Departing from the conventional noisy-channel approach of Brown et al. (1993), our basic model is a *direct* one:

$$c^* = \operatorname*{argmax}_c \Pr(c \mid e) \tag{2}$$

where e is the English input string and c^* is the best Chinese translation according to the translation model $\Pr(c \mid e)$. We now marginalize over all English parse trees $\mathcal{T}(e)$ that yield the sentence e:

$$\begin{aligned} \Pr(c \mid e) &= \sum_{\tau \in \mathcal{T}(e)} \Pr(\tau, c \mid e) \\ &= \sum_{\tau \in \mathcal{T}(e)} \Pr(\tau \mid e) \Pr(c \mid \tau) \end{aligned} \tag{3}$$

Rather than taking the sum, we pick the best tree τ^* and factors the search into two separate steps: parsing (4) (a well-studied problem) and tree-to-string translation (5) (Section 5):

$$\tau^* = \operatorname*{argmax}_{\tau \in \mathcal{T}(e)} \Pr(\tau \mid e) \tag{4}$$

$$c^* = \operatorname*{argmax}_c \Pr(c \mid \tau^*) \tag{5}$$

In this sense, our approach can be considered as a Viterbi approximation of the computationally expensive joint search using (3) directly. Similarly, we now marginalize over all derivations

$$\mathcal{D}(\tau^*) = \{d \mid \mathcal{E}(d) = \tau^*\}$$

that translates English tree τ into some Chinese string and apply the Viterbi approximation again to search for the best derivation d^*:

$$c^* = \mathcal{C}(d^*) = \mathcal{C}(\operatorname*{argmax}_{d \in \mathcal{D}(\tau^*)} \Pr(d)) \tag{6}$$

Assuming different rules in a derivation are applied independently, we approximate $\Pr(d)$ as

$$\Pr(d) = \prod_{r \in d} \Pr(r) \tag{7}$$

where the probability $\Pr(r)$ of the rule r is estimated by conditioning on the root symbol $\rho(t(r))$:

$$\begin{aligned} \Pr(r) &= \Pr(t(r), s(r) \mid \rho(t(r))) \\ &= \frac{c(r)}{\sum_{r':\rho(t(r'))=\rho(t(r))} c(r')} \end{aligned} \tag{8}$$

where $c(r)$ is the count (or frequency) of rule r in the training data.

4.2 Log-Linear Model

Following Och and Ney (2002), we extend the direct model into a general log-linear framework in order to incorporate other features:

$$c^* = \operatorname*{argmax}_c \Pr(c \mid e)^\alpha \cdot \Pr(c)^\beta \cdot e^{-\lambda |c|} \tag{9}$$

where $\Pr(c)$ is the language model and $e^{-\lambda|c|}$ is the length penalty term based on $|c|$, the length of the translation. Parameters α, β, and λ are the weights of relevant features. Note that positive λ prefers longer translations. We use a standard trigram model for $\Pr(c)$.

5 Search Algorithms

We first present a linear-time algorithm for searching the best derivation under the direct model, and then extend it to the log-linear case by a new variant of k-best parsing.

5.1 Direct Model: Memoized Recursion

Since our probability model is not based on the noisy channel, we do not call our search module a "decoder" as in most statistical MT work. Instead, readers who speak English but not Chinese can view it as an "encoder" (or encryptor), which corresponds exactly to our *direct* model.

Given a fixed parse-tree τ^*, we are to search for the best derivation with the highest probability. This can be done by a simple top-down traversal (or depth-first search) from the root of τ^*: at each node η in τ^*, try each possible rule r whose English-side pattern $t(r)$ matches the subtree τ^*_η rooted at η, and recursively visit each descendant node η_i in τ^*_η that corresponds to a variable in $t(r)$. We then collect the resulting target-language strings and plug them into the Chinese-side $s(r)$ of rule r, getting a translation for the subtree τ^*_η. We finally take the best of all translations.

With the extended LHS of our transducer, there may be many different rules applicable at one tree node. For example, consider the VP subtree in Fig. 3 (c), where both r_3 and r_6 can apply. As a result, the number of derivations is exponential in the size of the tree, since there are exponentially many decompositions of the tree for a given set of rules. This problem can be solved by *memoization* (Cormen et al., 2001): we cache each subtree that has been visited before, so that every tree node is visited *at most* once. This results in a dynamic programming algorithm that is guaranteed to run in $O(npq)$ time where n is the size of the parse tree, p is the maximum number of rules applicable to one tree node, and q is the maximum size of an applicable rule. For a given rule-set, this algorithm runs in time linear to the length of the input sentence, since p and q are considered grammar constants, and n is proportional to the input length. The full pseudo-code is worked out in Algorithm 1. A restricted version of this algorithm first appears in compiling for optimal code generation from expression-trees (Aho and Johnson, 1976). In computational linguistics, the bottom-up version of this algorithm resembles the *tree parsing* algorithm for TSG by Eisner (2003). Similar algorithms have also been proposed for dependency-based translation (Lin, 2004; Ding and Palmer, 2005).

5.2 Log-linear Model: k-best Search

Under the log-linear model, one still prefers to search for the globally best derivation d^*:

$$d^* = \operatorname*{argmax}_{d \in \mathcal{D}(\tau^*)} \Pr(d)^{\alpha} \Pr(\mathcal{C}(d))^{\beta} e^{-\lambda|\mathcal{C}(d)|} \quad (10)$$

However, integrating the n-gram model with the translation model in the search is computationally very expensive. As a standard alternative, rather than aiming at the exact best derivation, we search for top-k derivations under the direct model using Algorithm 1, and then rerank the k-best list with the language model and length penalty.

Like other instances of dynamic programming, Algorithm 1 can be viewed as a hypergraph search problem. To this end, we use an efficient algorithm by Huang and Chiang (2005, Algorithm 3) that solves the general k-best derivations problem in monotonic hypergraphs. It consists of a normal forward phase for the 1-best derivation and a recursive backward phase for the 2nd, 3rd, ..., k^{th} derivations.

Unfortunately, different derivations may have the same yield (a problem called *spurious ambiguity*), due to multi-level LHS of our rules. In practice, this results in a very small ratio of unique strings among top-k derivations. To alleviate this problem, determinization techniques have been proposed by Mohri and Riley (2002) for finite-state automata and extended to tree automata by May and Knight (2006). These methods eliminate spurious ambiguity by effectively transforming the grammar into an equivalent deterministic form. However, this transformation often leads to a blow-up in forest size, which is exponential to the original size in the worst-case.

So instead of determinization, here we present a simple-yet-effective extension to the Algorithm 3 of Huang and Chiang (2005) that guarantees to output unique translated strings:

- keep a hash-table of unique strings at each vertex in the hypergraph
- when asking for the next-best derivation of a vertex, keep asking until we get a new string, and then add it into the hash-table

This method should work in general for any equivalence relation (say, same derived tree) that can be defined on derivations.

6 Experiments

Our experiments are on English-to-Chinese translation, the opposite direction to most of the recent work in SMT. We are not doing the reverse direction at this time partly due to the lack of a sufficiently good parser for Chinese.

6.1 Data Preparation

Our training set is a Chinese-English parallel corpus with 1.95M aligned sentences (28.3M words on the English side). We first word-align them by GIZA++, then parse the English side by a variant of Collins (1999) parser, and finally apply the rule-extraction algorithm of Galley et al. (2004). The resulting rule set has 24.7M **xRs** rules. We also use the SRI Language Modeling Toolkit (Stolcke, 2002) to train a Chinese trigram model with Knesser-Ney smoothing on the Chinese side of the parallel corpus.

Our evaluation data consists of 140 short sentences (< 25 Chinese words) of the Xinhua portion of the NIST 2003 Chinese-to-English evaluation set. Since we are translating in the other direction, we use the first English reference as the source input and the Chinese as the single reference.

Algorithm 1 Top-down Memoized Recursion

```
function TRANSLATE(η)
    if cache[η] defined then                                  ▷ this sub-tree visited before?
        return cache[η]
    best ← 0
    for r ∈ R do                                              ▷ try each rule r
        matched, sublist ← PATTERNMATCH(t(r), η)              ▷ tree pattern matching
        if matched then                 ▷ if matched, sublist contains a list of matched subtrees
            prob ← Pr(r)                                      ▷ the probability of rule r
            for η_i ∈ sublist do
                p_i, s_i ← TRANSLATE(η_i)                     ▷ recursively solve each sub-problem
                prob ← prob · p_i
            if prob > best then
                best ← prob
                str ← [x_i ↦ s_i]s(r)                         ▷ plug in the results
    cache[η] ← best, str                                      ▷ caching the best solution for future use
    return cache[η]                                           ▷ returns the best string with its prob.
```

6.2 Initial Results

We implemented our system as follows: for each input sentence, we first run Algorithm 1, which returns the 1-best translation and also builds the derivation forest of all translations for this sentence. Then we extract the top 5000 non-duplicate translated strings from this forest and rescore them with the trigram model and the length penalty.

We compared our system with a state-of-the-art phrase-based system Pharaoh (Koehn, 2004) on the evaluation data. Since the target language is Chinese, we report character-based BLEU score instead of word-based to ensure our results are independent of Chinese tokenizations (although our language models are word-based). The BLEU scores are based on single reference and up to 4-gram precisions (r1n4). Feature weights of both systems are tuned on the same data set.[3] For Pharaoh, we use the standard minimum error-rate training (Och, 2003); and for our system, since there are only two independent features (as we always fix $\alpha = 1$), we use a simple grid-based line-optimization along the language-model weight axis. For a given language-model weight β, we use binary search to find the best length penalty λ that leads to a length-ratio closest to 1 against the reference. The results are summarized in Table 1. The rescored translations are better than the 1-best results from the direct model, but still slightly worse than Pharaoh.

Table 1: BLEU (r1n4) score results

system	BLEU
Pharaoh	25.5
direct model (1-best)	20.3
log-linear model (rescored 5000-best)	23.8

7 Conclusion and On-going Work

This paper presents an adaptation of the classic syntax-directed translation with linguistically-motivated formalisms for statistical MT. Currently we are doing larger-scale experiments. We are also investigating more principled algorithms for integrating n-gram language models during the search, rather than k-best rescoring. Besides, we will extend this work to translating the top k parse trees, instead of committing to the 1-best tree, as parsing errors certainly affect translation quality.

[3]In this sense, we are only reporting performances on the development set at this point. We will report results tuned and tested on separate data sets in the final version of this paper.

References

A. V. Aho and S. C. Johnson. 1976. Optimal code generation for expression trees. *J. ACM*, 23(3):488–501.

Alfred V. Aho and Jeffrey D. Ullman. 1972. *The Theory of Parsing, Translation, and Compiling*, volume I: Parsing. Prentice Hall, Englewood Cliffs, New Jersey.

Hiyan Alshawi, Srinivas Bangalore, and Shona Douglas. 2000. Learning dependency translation models as collections of finite state head transducers. *Computational Linguistics*, 26(1):45–60.

Peter F. Brown, Stephen A. Della Pietra, Vincent J. Della Pietra, and Robert L. Mercer. 1993. The mathematics of statistical machine translation: Parameter estimation. *Computational Linguistics*, 19:263–311.

Eugene Charniak. 2000. A maximum-entropy-inspired parser. In *Proc. of NAACL*, pages 132–139.

David Chiang. 2005. A hierarchical phrase-based model for statistical machine translation. In *Proc. of the 43rd ACL*.

Michael Collins. 1999. *Head-Driven Statistical Models for Natural Language Parsing*. Ph.D. thesis, University of Pennsylvania.

Thomas H. Cormen, Charles E. Leiserson, Ronald L. Rivest, and Clifford Stein. 2001. *Introduction to Algorithms*. MIT Press, second edition.

Yuan Ding and Martha Palmer. 2005. Machine translation using probablisitic synchronous dependency insertion grammars. In *Proceedings of the 43rd ACL*.

Jason Eisner. 2003. Learning non-isomorphic tree mappings for machine translation. In *Proceedings of ACL (companion volume)*, pages 205–208.

Heidi J. Fox. 2002. Phrasal cohesion and statistical machine translation. In *In Proc. of EMNLP*.

Michel Galley, Mark Hopkins, Kevin Knight, and Daniel Marcu. 2004. What's in a translation rule? In *HLT-NAACL*.

F. Gécseg and M. Steinby. 1984. *Tree Automata*. Akadémiai Kiadó, Budapest.

Jonathan Graehl and Kevin Knight. 2004. Training tree transducers. In *HLT-NAACL*, pages 105–112.

Liang Huang and David Chiang. 2005. Better k-best Parsing. In *Proceedings of the Nineth International Workshop on Parsing Technologies (IWPT-2005), 9-10 October 2005, Vancouver, Canada*.

E. T. Irons. 1961. A syntax-directed compiler for ALGOL 60. *Comm. ACM*, 4(1):51–55.

Aravind Joshi and Yves Schabes. 1997. Tree-adjoining grammars. In G. Rozenberg and A. Salomaa, editors, *Handbook of Formal Languages*, volume 3, pages 69 – 124. Springer, Berlin.

Philipp Koehn, Franz Joseph Och, and Daniel Marcu. 2003. Statistical phrase-based translation. In *Proc. of HLT-NAACL*, pages 127–133.

Philipp Koehn. 2004. Pharaoh: a beam search decoder for phrase-based statistical machine translation models. In *Proc. of AMTA*, pages 115–124.

Shankar Kumar and William Byrne. 2003. A weighted finite state transducer implementation of the alignment template model for statistical machine translation. In *Proc. of HLT-NAACL*, pages 142–149.

P. M. Lewis and R. E. Stearns. 1968. Syntax-directed transduction. *Journal of the ACM*, 15(3):465–488.

Dekang Lin. 2004. A path-based transfer model for machine translation. In *Proceedings of the 20th COLING*.

Jonathan May and Kevin Knight. 2006. A better n-best list: Practical determinization of weighted finite tree automata. Submitted to HLT-NAACL 2006.

Mehryar Mohri and Michael Riley. 2002. An efficient algorithm for the n-best-strings problem. In *Proceedings of the International Conference on Spoken Language Processing 2002 (ICSLP '02)*, Denver, Colorado, September.

Franz Josef Och and Hermann Ney. 2002. Discriminative training and maximum entropy models for statistical machine translation. In *Proc. of ACL*.

F. J. Och and H. Ney. 2004. The alignment template approach to statistical machine translation. *Computational Linguistics*, 30:417–449.

Franz Och. 2003. Minimum error rate training for statistical machine translation. In *Proc. of ACL*.

Chris Quirk, Arul Menezes, and Colin Cherry. 2005. Dependency treelet translation: Syntactically informed phrasal smt. In *Proceedings of the 43rd ACL*.

Stuart Shieber and Yves Schabes. 1990. Synchronous tree-adjoining grammars. In *Proc. of COLING*, pages 253–258.

Andrea Stolcke. 2002. Srilm: an extensible language modeling toolkit. In *Proc. of ICSLP*.

Dekai Wu. 1997. Stochastic inversion transduction grammars and bilingual parsing of parallel corpora. *Computational Linguistics*, 23(3):377–404.

Kenji Yamada and Kevin Knight. 2001. A syntax-based statistical translation model. In *Proc. of ACL*.

Efficient Dynamic Programming Search Algorithms for Phrase-Based SMT

Christoph Tillmann
IBM T.J. Watson Research Center
Yorktown Heights, NY 10598
ctill@us.ibm.com

Abstract

This paper presents a series of efficient dynamic-programming (DP) based algorithms for phrase-based decoding and alignment computation in statistical machine translation (SMT). The DP-based decoding algorithms are analyzed in terms of shortest path-finding algorithms, where the similarity to DP-based decoding algorithms in speech recognition is demonstrated. The paper contains the following original contributions: 1) the DP-based decoding algorithm in (Tillmann and Ney, 2003) is extended in a formal way to handle phrases and a novel pruning strategy with increased translation speed is presented 2) a novel alignment algorithm is presented that computes a phrase alignment efficiently in the case that it is consistent with an underlying word alignment. Under certain restrictions, both algorithms handle MT-related problems efficiently that are generally NP complete (Knight, 1999).

1 Introduction

This paper deals with dynamic programming based decoding and alignment algorithms for phrase-based SMT. Dynamic Programming based search algorithms are being used in speech recognition (Jelinek, 1998; Ney et al., 1992) as well as in statistical machine translation (Tillmann et al., 1997; Niessen et al., 1998; Tillmann and Ney, 2003). Here, the decoding algorithms are described as shortest path finding algorithms in regularly structured search graphs or search grids. Under certain restrictions, e.g. start and end point restrictions for the path, the shortest path computed corresponds to a recognized word sequence or a generated target language translation. In these algorithms, a shortest-path search is carried out in one pass over some input along a specific 'direction': in speech recognition the search is time-synchronous, the single-word based search algorithm in (Tillmann et al., 1997) is (source) position-synchronous or left-to-right, the search algorithm in (Niessen et al., 1998) is (target) position-synchronous or bottom-to-top, and the search algorithm in (Tillmann and Ney, 2003) is so-called cardinality-synchronous.

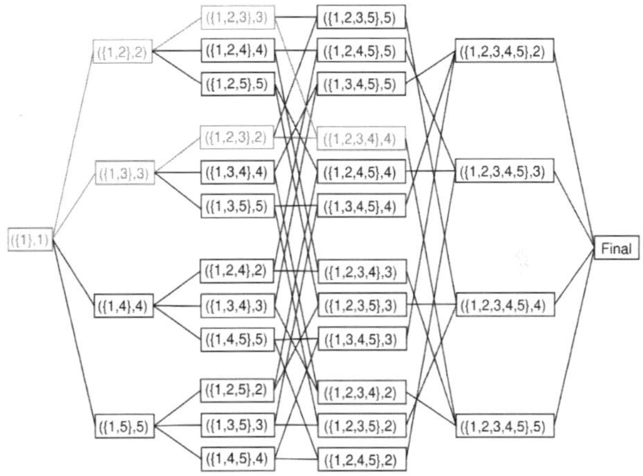

Figure 1: Illustration of a DP-based algorithm to solve a traveling salesman problem with 5 cities. The visited cities correspond to processed source positions.

Taking into account the different word order between source and target language sentences, it becomes less obvious that a SMT search algorithm can be described as a shortest path finding algorithm. But this has been shown by linking decoding to a dynamic-programming solution for the traveling salesman problem. This algorithm due to (Held and Karp, 1962) is a special case of a shortest path finding algorithm (Dreyfus and Law, 1977). The regularly structured search graph for this problem is illustrated in Fig. 1: all paths from the left-most to the right-most vertex correspond to a translation of the in-

Workshop on Computationally Hard Problemsand Joint Inference in Speech and Language Processing, pages 9–16,
New York City, New York, June 2006. ©2006 Association for Computational Linguistics

put sentence, where each source position is processed exactly once. In this paper, the DP-based search algorithm in (Tillmann and Ney, 2003) is extended in a formal way to handle phrase-based translation. Two versions of a phrase-based decoder for SMT that search slightly different search graphs are presented: a multi-beam decoder reported in the literature and a single-beam decoder with increased translation speed [1]. A common analysis of all the search algorithms above in terms of a shortest-path finding algorithm for a directed acyclic graph (**dag**) is presented. This analysis provides a simple way of analyzing the complexity of DP-based search algorithm.

Generally, the regular search space can only be fully searched for small search grids under appropriate restrictions, i.e. the monotonicity restrictions in (Tillmann et al., 1997) or the inverted search graph in (Niessen et al., 1998). For larger search spaces as are required for continuous speech recognition (Ney et al., 1992) [2] or phrase-based decoding in SMT, the search space cannot be fully searched: suitably defined lists of path hypothesis are maintained that partially explore the search space. The number of hypotheses depends locally on the number hypotheses whose score is close to the top scoring hypothesis: this set of hypotheses is called the beam.

The translation model used in this paper is a phrase-based model, where the translation units are so-called blocks: a block is a pair of phrases which are translations of each other. For example, Fig. 2 shows an Arabic-English translation example that uses 5 blocks. During decoding, we view translation as a block segmentation process, where the input sentence is segmented from left to right and the target sentence is generated from bottom to top, one block at a time. In practice, a largely monotone block sequence is generated except for the possibility to swap some neighbor blocks. During decoding, we try to minimize the score $s_w(b_1^n)$ of a block sequence b_1^n under the restriction that the concatenated source phrases of the blocks b_i yield a segmentation of the input sentence:

$$s_w(b_1^n) \;=\; \sum_{i=1}^{n} c(b_{i-1}, b_i) = \sum_{i=1}^{n} w^T \cdot f(b_{i-1}, b_i). \quad (1)$$

Here, $f(b_{i-1}, b_i)$ is 7-dimensional feature vector with real-valued features and w is the corresponding weight vector as described in Section 5. The fact that a given block covers some source interval $[j', j]$ is implicit in this notation.

[1]The multi-beam decoder is similar to the decoder presented in (Koehn, 2004) which is a standard decoder used in phrase-based SMT. A multi-beam decoder is also used in (Al-Onaizan et al., 2004) and (Berger et al., 1996).

[2]In that work, there is a distinction between within-word and between-word search, which is not relevant for phrase-based decoding where only exact phrase matches are searched.

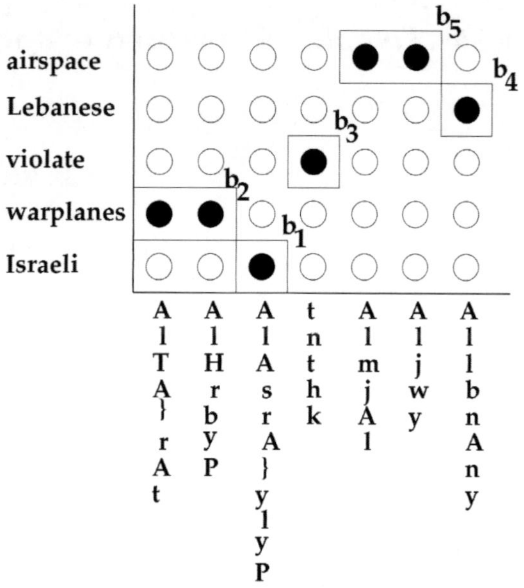

Figure 2: An Arabic-English block translation example, where the Arabic words are romanized. A sequence of 5 blocks is generated.

This paper is structured as follows: Section 2 introduces the multi-beam and the single-beam DP-based decoders. Section 3 presents an analysis of all the graph-based shortest-path finding algorithm mentioned above: a search algorithm for a directed acyclic graph (**dag**). Section 4 shows an efficient phrasal alignment algorithm that gives an algorithmic justification for learning blocks from word-aligned training. Finally, Section 5 presents an evaluation of the beam-search decoders on an Arabic-English decoding task.

2 Beam-Search Decoding Algorithms

In this section, we introduce two beam-search algorithms for SMT: a multi-beam algorithm and single-beam algorithm. The multi-beam search algorithm is presented first, since it is conceptually simpler.

2.1 Multi-Beam Decoder

For the multi-beam decoder makes use of search states that are 3-tuples of the following type:

$$[\, C \,,\, h \,;\, d \,]. \quad (2)$$

h is the state history, that depends on the block generation model. In our case, $h = ([j, j'], [u, v])$, where $([j, j'])$ is the interval where the most recent block matched the input sentence, and $[u, v]$ are the final two target words of the partial translation produced thus far. C is the so-called coverage vector that ensures that a consistent block alignment is obtained during decoding and that the decoding

Table 1: Multi-beam (M-**Beam**) decoding algorithm, which is similar to (Koehn, 2004). The decoders differ in their pruning strategy: here, each state list Γ_c is pruned only once, whereas the decoder in (Koehn, 2004) prunes a state list every time a new hypothesis is entered.

input: source sentence with words $f_1, \cdots, f_J$

$\Gamma_0 := \{\sigma_0\}$ and $\Gamma_k := \emptyset$ for $k = 1, \cdots, J$
for each $c = 0, 1, \cdots, J$ **do**
    Prune state set Γ_c
    for each state σ in Γ_c **do**
        matcher: for each $\sigma' : \sigma \rightarrow_M \sigma'$
            update σ' for $\Gamma_{c+l(\sigma')}$
    end
end

output: translation from lowest cost state in Γ_J

can be carried out efficiently. It keeps track of the already processed input sentence positions. d is the cost of the shortest path (distance) from some initial state σ_0 to the current state σ. The baseline decoder maintains $J + 1$ state lists with entries of the above type, where J is the number of input words. The states are stored in lists or stacks that support lookup operations to check whether a given state tuple is already present in a list and what its score d is.

The use of a coverage vector $\mathcal{C}$ is related to a DP-based solution for the traveling salesman problem as illustrated in Fig. 1. The algorithm keeps track of sets of visited cities along with the identity of the last visited city. Cities correspond to source sentence positions j. The vertexes in this graph correspond to set of already visited cities. Since the traveling salesman problem (and also the translation model) uses only local costs, the order in which the source positions have been processed can be ignored. Conceptually, the re-ordering problem is **linearized** by searching a path through the set inclusion graph in Fig. 1. Phrase-based decoding is handle by an almost identical algorithm: the last visited position j is replaced by an interval $[j', j]$.

The states are stored in lists or stacks that support lookup operations to check whether a given state tuple is already present in a list and what its score d is. Extending the partial block translation that is represented by a state σ with a single block b' generates a new state σ'. Here, $[k, k']$ is the source interval where block b' matches the input sentence. The state transition is defined as follows:

$$[\mathcal{C}\,,\, h\,;\, d] \;\; \rightarrow_M \;\; [\mathcal{C}'\,,\, h'\,;\, d']\,. \tag{3}$$

The σ' state fields are updated on a component-by-component basis. $\mathcal{C}' = \mathcal{C} \cup [k, k']$ is the coverage vector obtained by adding all the positions from the interval $[k, k']$. The new state history is defined as $h' = ([k, k'], [u', v'])$ where u' and v' are the final two target words of the target phrase T' of b'. Some special cases, e.g. where T' has less than two target words, are taken into account. The path cost d' is computed as $d' = d + d(\sigma, \sigma')$, where the transition cost $d(\sigma, \sigma') := c(b, b')$ is computed from the history h and the matching block b' as defined in Section 5.

Table 2: Single-beam (S-**Beam**) decoding algorithm (related to (Lowerre and Reddy, 1980)).

input: source sentence with words $f_1, \cdots, f_J$

$\Gamma := \{\sigma_0\}$
for each $c = 0, 1, \cdots, J$ **do**
    $\Gamma' := \{\emptyset\}$
    for each state σ in Γ **do**
        if CLOSED?(σ) **then**
            matcher: for each $\sigma' : \sigma \rightarrow_M \sigma'$
        else
            scanner: for single $\sigma' : \sigma \rightarrow_S \sigma'$
        update σ' **for** Γ'
        end
    Prune state set Γ'
    Swap Γ, Γ'
    end
end

output: translation from lowest cost state in Γ

The decoder in Table 1 fills $J + 1$ state sets $\Gamma_k : k = \{0, \cdots, J\}$. All the coverage vectors $\mathcal{C}$ for states in the set Γ_k cover the same number of source positions k. When a state set Γ_k is processed, the decoder has finished processing all states in the sets Γ_l where $l < k$. Before expanding a state set, the decoder prunes a state set based on its coverage vector and the path costs only: two different pruning strategies are used that have been introduced in (Tillmann and Ney, 2003): 1) **coverage pruning** prunes states that share the same coverage vector $\mathcal{C}$, 2) **cardinality pruning** prunes states according to the cardinality $c(\mathcal{C})$ of covered positions: all states in the beam are compared with each other. Since the states are kept in $J + 1$ separate lists, which are pruned independently of each others, this decoder version is called **multi-beam** decoder. The decoder uses a **matcher** function when expanding a state: for a state σ it looks for uncovered source positions to find source phrase matches for blocks. **Updating** a state in Table 1 includes adding the state if it is not yet present or updating its shortest path cost d: if the state is already in Γ_c only the state with the lower path cost d is kept. This inserting/updating operation is also called **recombination** or **relaxation** in the context of a dag search algorithm (cf. Section 3). The **update** procedure also stores for each state σ' its predecessor state in a so-called back-pointer array (Ney et al., 1992). The final block alignment and target translation can be recovered from this back-pointer array once the final state set Γ_J has been computed. $l(\sigma')$ is the source phrase length of the matching block b' when going from σ to σ'. This algorithm is similar to the beam-search algorithm presented in (Koehn, 2004): it allows states to be added to a stack that is not the stack for the successor cardinality. σ_0 is the initial decoder state, where no source position is covered: $\mathcal{C} = \emptyset$. For the final states in Γ_J all source positions are covered.

2.2 Single-Beam Implementation

The second implementation uses two lists to keep a single beam of active states. This corresponds to a beam-search decoder in speech recognition, where path hypotheses corresponding to word sequences are processed in a time-synchronous way and at a given time step only hypotheses within some percentage of the best hypothesis are kept (Lowerre and Reddy, 1980). The single-beam decoder processes hypotheses **cardinality-synchronously**, i.e. the states at stage k generate new states at position $k+1$. In order to make the use of a single beam possible, we slightly modify the state transitions in Eq. 3:

$$[\mathcal{C}\,,\, l\,,\, h\,;\, d] \quad \to_S \quad [\mathcal{C}'\,,\, l'\,,\, h\,;\, d']\,, \qquad (4)$$

$$[\mathcal{C}\,,\, \cdot\,, h\,;\, d] \quad \to_M \quad [\mathcal{C}'\,,\, l' = k\,,\, h'\,;\, d']\,. \qquad (5)$$

Here, Eq. 5 corresponds to the matcher definition in Eq. 3. We add an additional field that is a pointer keeping track of how much of the recent source phrase match has been covered. In Eq. 5, when a block is matched to the input sentence, this pointer is set to position k where the most recent block match starts. We use a dot $\cdot$ to indicate that when a block is matched, the matching position of the predecessor state can be ignored. While the pointer l is not yet equal to the end position of the match k', it is increased $l' := l + 1$ as shown in Eq. 4. The path cost d is set: $d' = d + \Delta$, where Δ is the state transition cost $d(\sigma, \sigma')$ divided by the source phrase length of block b': we evenly spread the cost of generating b' over all source positions being matched. The new coverage vector $\mathcal{C}'$ is obtained from $\mathcal{C}$ by adding the scanned position l': $\mathcal{C}' = \mathcal{C} \cup \{l'\}$. The algorithm that makes use of the above definitions is shown in Table 2. The states are stored in only two state sets Γ and Γ': Γ contains the most probable hypotheses that were kept in the last beam pruning step all of which cover k source positions. Γ' contains all the hypotheses in the current beam that cover $k+1$ source positions. The single-beam decoder in Table 2 uses two procedures: the **scanner** and the **matcher** correspond to the state transitions in Eq. 4 and Eq. 5. Here, the **matcher** simply matches a block to an uncovered portion of the input sentence. After the matcher has matched a block, that block is processed in a cardinality-synchronous way using the scanner procedure as described above. The predicate CLOSED?(σ) is used to switch between matching and scanning states. The predicate CLOSED?(σ) is true if the pointer l is equal to the match end position k' (this is stored in h'). At this point, the position-by-position match of the source phrase is completed and we can search for additional block matches.

3 DP Shortest Path Algorithm for dag

This section analyzes the relationship between the block decoding algorithms in this paper and a single-source shortest path finding algorithm for a directed acyclic graphs (dag). We closely follow the presentation in (Cormen et al., 2001) and only sketch the algorithm here: a dag $G = (V, E)$ is a weighted graph for which a topological sort of its vertex set V exists: all the vertexes can be enumerated in linear order. For such a weighted graph, the shortest path from a single source can be computed in $O(|V| + |E|)$ time, where $|V|$ is the number of vertexes and $|E|$ number of edges in the graph. The dag search algorithm runs over all vertexes σ in topological order. Assuming an **adjacency-list** representation of the dag, for each vertex σ, we loop over all successor vertexes σ', where each vertex σ with its adjacency-list is processed exactly once. During the search, we maintain for each vertex σ' an attribute $d[\sigma']$, which is an upper bound on the shortest path cost from the source vertex s to the vertex σ'. This shortest path estimate is updated or **relaxed** each time the vertex σ' occurs in some adjacency list. Ignoring the pruning, the M-Beam decoding algorithm in Table 1 and the dag search algorithm can be compared as follows: states correspond to dag vertexes and state transitions correspond to dag edges. Using two loops for the multi-beam decoder while generating states in stages is just a way of generating a topological sort of the search states on the fly: a linear order of search states is generated by appending the search states in the state lists Γ_0, Γ_1, etc. .

The analysis in terms of a dag shortest path algorithm can be used for a simple complexity analysis of the proposed algorithms. Local state transitions correspond to an adjacency-list traversal in the dag search algorithm. These involve costly lookup operations, e.g. language, distortion and translation model probability lookup. Typically the computation time for update operations on lists Γ is negligible compared to these probability lookups. So, the search algorithm complexity is simply computed as the number of edges in the search graph: $O(|V| + |E|) \approx O(|E|)$ (this analysis is implicit in (Tillmann,

2001)). Without proof, for the search algorithm in Section 2.1 we observe that the number of states is finite and that all the states are actually reachable from the start state σ_0. This way for the single-word based search in (Tillmann and Ney, 2003), a complexity of $O(|V_T|^3 \cdot J^2 \cdot 2^J)$ is shown, where $|V_T|$ is the size of the target vocabulary and J is the length of the input sentence. The complexity is dominated by the exponential number of coverage vectors C that occur in the search, and the complexity of phrase-based decoding is higher yet since its hypotheses store a source interval $[j', j]$ rather than a single source position j. In the general case, no efficient search algorithm exists to search all word or phrase re-orderings (Knight, 1999). Efficient search algorithms can be derived by the restricting the allowable coverage vectors (Tillmann, 2001) to local word re-ordering only. An efficient phrase alignment method that does not make use of re-ordering restriction is demonstrated in the following section.

4 Efficient Block Alignment Algorithm

A common approach to phrase-based SMT is to learn phrasal translation pairs from word-aligned training data (Och and Ney, 2004). Here, a word alignment $\mathcal{A}$ is a subset of the Cartesian product of source and target positions:

$$\mathcal{A} \subseteq \{1, \cdots, I\} \times \{1, \cdots, J\}.$$

Here, I is the target sentence length and J is the source sentence length. The phrase learning approach in (Och and Ney, 2004) takes two alignments: a source-to-target alignment $\mathcal{A}_1$ and a target-to-source alignment $\mathcal{A}_2$. The intersection of these two alignments is computed to obtain a high-precision word alignment. Here, we note that if the intersection covers all source and target positions (as shown in Fig. 4), it constitutes a bijection between source and target sentence positions, since the intersecting alignments are functions according to their definition in (Brown et al., 1993) [3]. In this paper, an algorithmic justification for restricting blocks based on word alignments is given. We assume that source and target sentence are given, and the task is to compute the lowest scoring block alignment. Such an algorithm might be important in some discriminative training procedure that relies on decoding the training data efficiently.

To restrict the block selection based on word aligned training data, interval projection functions are defined as follows [4]: S is a source interval and T is an target interval. $proj_T(S)$ is the set of target positions i such that the alignment point (i, j) occurs in the alignment set $\mathcal{A}$ and j is covered by the source interval S. $proj_S(T)$ is defined accordingly. Formally, the definitions look like this:

$$\begin{aligned} proj_T(S) &= \{\, i \mid (i,j) \in \mathcal{A} \text{ and } j \in S \,\} \\ proj_S(T) &= \{\, j \mid (i,j) \in \mathcal{A} \text{ and } i \in T \,\} \end{aligned}$$

In order to obtain a particularly simple block alignment algorithm, the allowed block links (S, T) are restricted by an ADMISSIBILITY restriction, which is defined as follows:

$$(T, S) \text{ is admissible } \textbf{iff} \quad (6)$$
$$proj_S(T) \subseteq S \text{ and } proj_T(S) \subseteq T$$

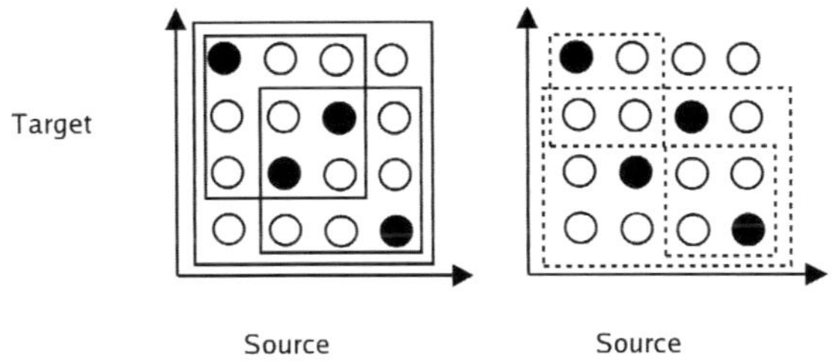

Figure 3: Following the definition in Eq. 6, the left picture shows three **admissible** block links while the right picture shows three **non-admissible** block links.

Admissibility is related to the word re-ordering problem: for the source positions in an interval S and for the target positions in an interval T, all word re-ordering involving these positions has to take place **within** the block defined by S and T. Without an underlying alignment $\mathcal{A}$ each pair of source and target intervals would define a possible block link: the admissibility reduces the number of block links drastically. Examples of admissible and non-admissible blocks are shown in Fig. 3.

If the alignment $\mathcal{A}$ is a bijection, by definition each target position i is aligned to exactly one source position j and vice versa and source and target sentence have the same length. Because of the admissibility definition, a target interval clumping alone is sufficient to determine the source interval clumping **and** the clump alignment. In Fig. 4, a bijection word alignment for a sentence pair that consists of $J = 4$ source and $I = 4$ target words is shown, where the alignment links that yield a bijection are shown as solid dots. Four admissible block alignments are shown as well. An admissible block alignment is always guaranteed to exist: the block that covers all source and target position is admissible by definition. The underlying word alignment and the admissibility restriction play together to reduce the number of block alignments: out of all eight possible target clumpings, only

[3](Tillmann, 2003) reports an intersection coverage of about 65 % for Arabic-English parallel data, and a coverage of 40 % for Chinese-English data. In the case of uncomplete coverage, the current algorithm can be extended as described in Section 4.1.

[4](Och and Ney, 2004) defines the notion of consistency for the set of phrasal translations that are learned from word-aligned training data which is equivalent.

Table 3: Efficient DP-based block alignment algorithm using an underlying word alignment $\mathcal{A}$. For simplicity reasons, the block score $c(b')$ is computed based on the block identity b' only.

input: Parallel sentence pair and alignment $\mathcal{A}$.
initialization: $Q(0) = 0$; $Q(i) = \infty$; $\gamma(i, i') = \infty$; for $i, i' = 1, \cdots, I$.
for each $i = 1, 2, \cdots, I$ do
  $Q(i) = \min_{i'} \gamma(i, i') + Q(i')$, where
  $\gamma(i, i') = c(b')$ if block b' results from admissible block link (T, S), where $T = [i' + 1, i]$
traceback:
  - find best end hypothesis: $Q(I)$

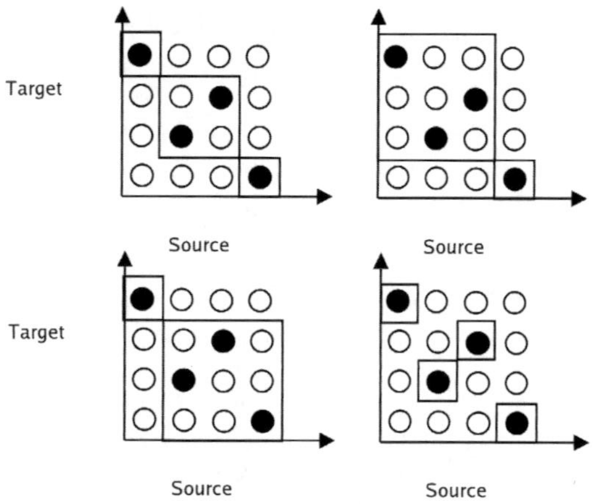

Figure 4: Four admissible block alignments in case the word alignment intersection is a bijection. The block alignment which covers the whole sentence pair with a single block is not shown.

five yield segmentations with admissible block links. The DP-based algorithm to compute the block sequence with the highest score $Q(i)$ is shown in Table 3. Here, the following auxiliary quantity is used:

$Q(i) :=$ score of the best partial segmentation that covers the target interval $[1, i]$.

Target intervals are processed from bottom to top. A target interval $T = [i', i]$ is projected using the word alignment $\mathcal{A}$, where a given target interval might not yield an admissible block. For the initialization, we set $Q(i) = \infty$ and the final score is obtained as $Q_{Final} = Q(I)$. The complexity of the algorithm is $\mathcal{O}(I^2)$ where the time to compute the cost $c(b')$ and the time to compute the interval projections are ignored. Using the alignment links $\mathcal{A}$, the segmentation problem is essentially linearized: the target clumping is generated sequentially from bottom-to-top and it induces some source clumping in an order which is defined by the word alignment.

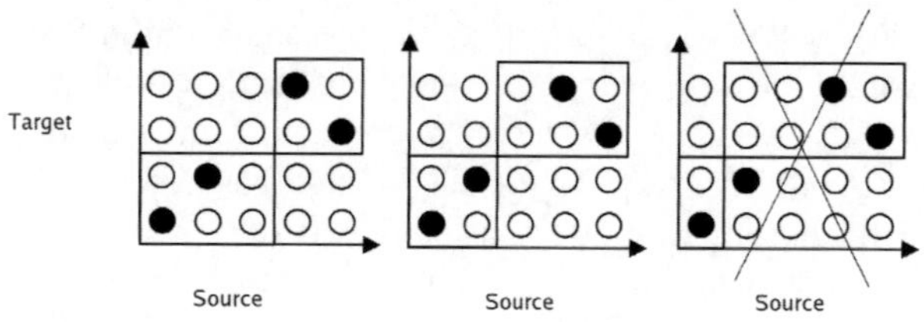

Figure 5: An example for a block alignment involving a non-aligned column. The right-most alignment is not allowed by the closure restriction.

4.1 Incomplete Bijection Coverage

In this section, an algorithm is sketched that works if the intersection coverage is not complete. In this case, a given target interval may produce several admissible block links since it can be coupled with different source intervals to form admissible block links, e.g. in Fig. 5, the target interval $[0, 1]$ is linked to two source intervals and both resulting block links do not violate the admissibility restriction. The minimum score block translation can be computed using either the one-beam or the multi-beam algorithm presented earlier. The search state definition in Eq. 2 is modified to keep track of the current target position i the same way as the recursive quantity $Q(i)$ does this in the algorithm in Table 3:

$$[\, \mathcal{C} \, , \, h \, , \, i \, ; \, d \,] \, . \tag{7}$$

Additionally, a complex block history h as defined in Section 2 can be used. Before the search is carried out, the set of admissible block links for each target interval is pre-computed and stored in a table where a simple look-up for each target interval $[i', i]$ is carried out during alignment. The efficiency of the block alignment algorithm depends on the alignment intersection coverage.

5 Beam-Search Results

In this section, we present results for the beam-search algorithms introduced in Section 2. The MT03 Arabic-English NIST evaluation test set consisting of 663 sentences with 16 278 Arabic words is used for the experiments. Translation results in terms of uncased BLEU using 4 reference translations are reported in Table 4 and Table 5 for the single-beam (S-**Beam**) and the multi-beam (M-**Beam**) search algorithm. For all re-ordering experiments, the notion of skips is used (Tillmann and Ney, 2003) to restrict the phrase re-ordering: the number of skips restricts the number of holes in the coverage vector for a left-to-right traversal of the input sentence. All

Table 4: Effect of the skip parameter for the two search strategies. $t_c = 2.5, t_{\mathcal{C}} = 1.0$ and window width $w = 6$.

Skip	BLEU	CPU	BLEU	CPU
	S-**Beam**	[secs]	M-**Beam**	[secs]
0	40.7 ± 1.4	108	40.9 ± 1.5	116
1	44.1 ± 1.5	729	44.1 ± 1.6	2459
2	44.3 ± 1.6	4408	44.4 ± 1.6	8437
3	44.3 ± 1.6	7467	44.5 ± 1.6	10048

re-ordering takes place in a window of size $w = 6$, such that only local block re-ordering is handled.

The following block bigram scoring is used: a block pair $(b; b')$ with corresponding source phrase matches $([j, j'], [k, k'])$ is represented as a feature-vector $f(b; b') \in \mathbb{R}^7$. The feature-vector components are the negative logarithm of some probabilities as well as a word-penalty feature. The real-valued features include the following: a block translation score derived from phrase occurrence statistics (1), a trigram language model to predict target words $(2-3)$, a lexical weighting score for the block internal words (4), a distortion model $(5-6)$ as well as the negative target phrase length (7). The transition cost is computed as $c(b\ ,\ b') = w^T \cdot f(b; b')$, where $w \in \mathbb{R}^7$ is a weight vector that sums up to 1.0: $\sum_{i=1}^{7} w_i = 1.0$. The weights are trained using a procedure similar to (Och, 2003) on held-out test data. A block set of 9.5 million blocks, which are not filtered according to any particular test set is used, which has been generated by a phrase-pair selection algorithm similar to (Al-Onaizan et al., 2004). The training data is sentence-aligned consisting of 3.3 million training sentence pairs.

Beam-search results are presented in terms of two pruning thresholds: the coverage pruning threshold $t_{\mathcal{C}}$ and the cardinality pruning threshold t_c (Tillmann and Ney, 2003). To carry out the pruning, the minimum cost with respect to each coverage set $\mathcal{C}$ and cardinality c are computed for a state set Γ. For the coverage pruning, states are distinguished according to the subset of covered positions $\mathcal{C}$. The minimum cost $\hat{Q}_\Gamma(\mathcal{C})$ is defined as:$\hat{Q}_\Gamma(\mathcal{C}) = \min_d\{d \mid [\mathcal{C}, h; d] \in \Gamma\}$. For the cardinality pruning, states are distinguished according to the cardinality $c(\mathcal{C})$ of subsets $\mathcal{C}$ of covered positions. The minimum cost $\hat{Q}_\Gamma(c)$ is defined for all hypotheses with the same cardinality $c(\mathcal{C}) = c$: $\hat{Q}_\Gamma(c) = \min_{\substack{c \\ c(\mathcal{C})=c}} \hat{Q}_\Gamma(\mathcal{C})$.

States σ in Γ are pruned if the shortest path cost $d(\sigma)$ is greater than the minimum cost plus the pruning threshold:

$$\begin{aligned} d(\sigma) &> t_{\mathcal{C}} + \hat{Q}_\Gamma(\mathcal{C}) \\ d(\sigma) &> t_c + \hat{Q}_\Gamma(c) \end{aligned}$$

The same state set pruning is used for the S-Beam and the M-Beam search algorithms. Table 4 shows the effect of the skip size on the translation performance. The pruning thresholds are set to conservatively large values: $t_c = 2.5$ and $t_{\mathcal{C}} = 1.0$. Only if no block re-ordering is allowed ($skip = 0$), performance drops significantly. The S-Beam search is consistently faster than M-Beam search algorithm. Table 5 demonstrates the effect of the coverage pruning threshold. Here, a conservatively large cardinality pruning threshold of $t_c = 10.0$ and the so-called **histogram** pruning to restrict the overall number of states in the beam to a maximum number of 2500 are used to restrict the overall search space. The S-Beam search algorithm is consistently faster than the M-Beam search algorithm for the same pruning threshold, but performance in terms of BLEU score drops significantly for lower coverage pruning thresholds $t_{\mathcal{C}} < 0.5$ as a smaller portion of the overall search space is searched which leads to search errors. For larger pruning thresholds $t_{\mathcal{C}} \geq 0.5$, where the performance of the two algorithms in terms of BLEU score is nearly identical, the S-Beam algorithm runs significantly faster. For a coverage threshold of $t_{\mathcal{C}} = 0.1$, the S-Beam algorithm is as fast as the M-Beam algorithm at $t_{\mathcal{C}} = 0.01$, but obtains a significantly higher BLEU score of 42.6 versus 41.0 for the M-Beam algorithm. The results in this section show that the S-Beam algorithm generally runs faster since the beam search pruning is applied to all states simultaneously making more efficient use of the beam search concept.

Table 5: Effect of the coverage pruning threshold $t_{\mathcal{C}}$ on BLEU and the overall CPU time [secs]. To restrict the overall search space the cardinality pruning is set to $t_c = 10.0$ and the cardinality histogram pruning is set to 2500.

$t_{\mathcal{C}}$	BLEU	CPU	BLEU	CPU
	S-**Beam**	[secs]	M-**Beam**	[secs]
0.001	37.5 ± 1.4	106	40.5 ± 1.5	198
0.01	38.3 ± 1.4	109	41.0 ± 1.5	213
0.05	40.7 ± 1.5	139	43.2 ± 1.6	301
0.1	42.6 ± 1.5	215	44.2 ± 1.6	508
0.25	44.1 ± 1.6	1018	44.4 ± 1.6	1977
0.5	44.3 ± 1.6	4527	44.4 ± 1.6	6289
1.0	44.3 ± 1.6	6623	44.5 ± 1.6	8092
2.5	44.3 ± 1.6	6797	44.5 ± 1.6	8187
5.0	44.3 ± 1.6	6810	44.5 ± 1.6	8191

6 Discussion

The decoding algorithm shown here is most similar to the decoding algorithms presented in (Koehn, 2004) and (Och and Ney, 2004), the later being used for the Alignment Template Model for SMT. These algorithms also include an estimate of the path completion cost which can easily be included into this work as well ((Tillmann, 2001)). (Knight, 1999) shows that the decoding problem for SMT as well as some bilingual tiling problems are NP-complete, so no efficient algorithm exists in the general case. But using DP-based optimization techniques and appropriate restrictions leads to efficient DP-based decoding algorithms as shown in this paper.

The efficient block alignment algorithm in Section 4 is related to the inversion transduction grammar approach to bilingual parsing described in (Wu, 1997): in both cases the number of alignments is drastically reduced by introducing appropriate re-ordering restrictions. The list-based decoding algorithms can also be compared to an Earley-style parsing algorithm that processes list of parse states in a single left-to-right run over the input sentence. For this algorithm, the comparison in terms of a shortest-path algorithm is less obvious: in the so-called completion step the parser re-visits states in previous stacks. But it is interesting to note that there is no multiple lists variant of that parser. In phrase-based decoding, a multiple list decoder is feasible only because exact phrase matches occur. A block decoding algorithm that would allow for a 'fuzzy' match of source phrases, e.g. insertions or deletions of some source phrase words are allowed, would need to carry out its computations using two stacks since the match end of a block is unknown.

7 Acknowledgment

This work was partially supported by DARPA and monitored by SPAWAR under contract No. N66001-99-2-8916. The author would like to thank the anonymous reviewers for their detailed criticism on this paper.

References

Yaser Al-Onaizan, Niyu Ge, Young-Suk Lee, Kishore Papineni, Fei Xia, and Christoph Tillmann. 2004. IBM Site Report. In *NIST 2004 MT Workshop*, Alexandria, VA, June. IBM.

Adam L. Berger, Peter F. Brown, Stephen A. Della Pietra, Vincent J. Della Pietra, Andrew S. Kehler, and Robert L. Mercer. 1996. Language Translation Apparatus and Method of Using Context-Based Translation Models. *United States Patent, Patent Number 5510981*, April.

Peter F. Brown, Vincent J. Della Pietra, Stephen A. Della Pietra, and Robert L. Mercer. 1993. The Mathematics of Statistical Machine Translation: Parameter Estimation. *Computational Linguistics*, 19(2):263–311.

Thomas H. Cormen, Charles E. Leiserson, Ronald L. Rivest, and Clifford Stein. 2001. *Introduction to Algorithms*. MIT Press, Cambridge Massachusetts.

Stuart E. Dreyfus and Averill M. Law. 1977. *The Art and Theory of Dynamic Programming (Mathematics in Science and Engineering; vol. 130)*. Acadamic Press, New York, N.Y.

Held and Karp. 1962. A Dynamic Programming Approach to Sequencing Problems. *SIAM*, 10(1):196–210.

Fred Jelinek. 1998. *Statistical Methods for Speech Recognition*. The MIT Press, Cambridge, MA.

Kevin Knight. 1999. Decoding Complexity in Word-Replacement Translation Models. *CL*, 25(4):607–615.

Philipp Koehn. 2004. Pharaoh: a Beam Search Decoder for Phrase-Based Statistical Machine Translation Models. In *Proceedings of AMTA 2004*, Washington DC, September-October.

Bruce Lowerre and Raj Reddy. 1980. *The Harpy speech understanding system, in Trends in Speech Recognition, W.A. Lea, Ed.* Prentice Hall, EngleWood Cliffs, NJ.

H. Ney, D. Mergel, A. Noll, and A. Paeseler. 1992. Data Driven Search Organization for Continuous Speech Recognition in the SPICOS System. *IEEE Transaction on Signal Processing*, 40(2):272–281.

S. Niessen, S. Vogel, H. Ney, and C. Tillmann. 1998. A DP-Based Search Algorithm for Statistical Machine Translation. In *Proc. of ACL/COLING 98*, pages 960–967, Montreal, Canada, August.

Franz-Josef Och and Hermann Ney. 2004. The Alignment Template Approach to Statistical Machine Translation. *Computational Linguistics*, 30(4):417–450.

Franz Josef Och. 2003. Minimum error rate training in statistical machine translation. In *Proceedings of ACL'03*, pages 160–167, Sapporo, Japan.

Christoph Tillmann and Hermann Ney. 2003. Word Reordering and a DP Beam Search Algorithm for Statistical Machine Translation. *CL*, 29(1):97–133.

Christoph Tillmann, Stefan Vogel, Hermann Ney, and Alex Zubiaga. 1997. A DP-based Search Using Monotone Alignments in Statistical Translation. In *Proc. of ACL 97*, pages 289–296, Madrid,Spain, July.

Christoph Tillmann. 2001. *Word Re-Ordering and Dynamic Programming based Search Algorithm for Statistical Machine Translation*. Ph.D. thesis, University of Technology, Aachen, Germany.

Christoph Tillmann. 2003. A Projection Extension Algorithm for Statistical Machine Translation. In *Proc. of EMNLP 03*, pages 1–8, Sapporo, Japan, July.

Dekai Wu. 1997. Stochastic Inversion Transduction Grammars and Bilingual Parsing of Parallel Corpora. *Computational Linguistics*, 23(3):377–403.

Computational Challenges in Parsing by Classification

Joseph Turian and I. Dan Melamed
{lastname}@cs.nyu.edu
Computer Science Department
New York University
New York, New York 10003

Abstract

This paper presents a discriminative parser that does not use a generative model in any way, yet whose accuracy still surpasses a generative baseline. The parser performs feature selection incrementally during training, as opposed to *a priori*, which enables it to work well with minimal linguistic cleverness. The main challenge in building this parser was fitting the training data into memory. We introduce gradient sampling, which increased training speed 100-fold. Our implementation is freely available at http://nlp.cs.nyu.edu/parser/.

1 Introduction

Discriminative machine learning methods have improved accuracy on many NLP tasks, including POS-tagging, shallow parsing, relation extraction, and machine translation. However, only limited advances have been made on full syntactic constituent parsing. Successful discriminative parsers have used generative models to reduce training time and raise accuracy above generative baselines (Collins & Roark, 2004; Henderson, 2004; Taskar et al., 2004). However, relying upon information from a generative model might limit the potential of these approaches to realize the accuracy gains achieved by discriminative methods on other NLP tasks. Another difficulty is that discriminative parsing approaches can be very task-specific and require quite a bit of trial and error with different hyper-parameter values and types of features.

In the present work, we make progress towards overcoming these obstacles. We propose a flexible, well-integrated method for training discriminative parsers, demonstrating techniques that might also be useful for other structured learning problems. The learning algorithm projects the hand-provided atomic features into a compound feature space and performs incremental feature selection from this large feature space. We achieve higher accuracy than a generative baseline, despite not using the standard trick of including an underlying generative model. Our training regime does model selection without ad-hoc smoothing or frequency-based feature cutoffs, and requires no heuristics to optimize the single hyper-parameter.

We discuss the computational challenges we overcame to build this parser. The main difficulty is that the training data fit in memory only using an indirect representation,[1] so the most costly operation during training is accessing the features of a particular example. We show how to train a parser effectively under these conditions. We also show how to speed up training by using a principled sampling method to estimate the loss gradients used in feature selection.

§2 describes the parsing algorithm. §3 presents the learning method and techniques used to reduce training time. §4 presents experiments with discriminative parsers built using these methods. §5 dis-

[1]Similar memory limitations exist in other large-scale NLP tasks. Syntax-driven SMT systems are typically trained on an order of magnitude more sentences than English parsers, and unsupervised estimation methods can generate an arbitrary number of negative examples (Smith & Eisner, 2005).

Workshop on Computationally Hard Problemsand Joint Inference in Speech and Language Processing, pages 17–24,
New York City, New York, June 2006.

cusses possible issues in scaling to larger example sets.

2 Parsing Algorithm

The following terms will help to explain our work. A *span* is a range over contiguous words in the input. Spans *cross* if they overlap but neither contains the other. An *item* is a (span, label) pair. A *state* is a partial parse, i.e. a set of items, none of whose spans cross. A parse *inference* is a (state, item) pair, i.e. a state and a (consequent) item to be added to it. The *frontier* of a state consists of the items with no parents yet. The *children* of an inference are the frontier items below the item to be inferred, and the *head* of an inference is the child item chosen by head rules (Collins, 1999, pp. 238–240). A parse *path* is a sequence of parse inferences. For some input sentence and training parse tree, a state is *correct* if the parser can infer zero or more additional items to obtain the training parse tree and an inference is correct if it leads to a correct state.

Now, given input sentence s we compute:

$$\hat{p} = \arg\min_{p \in P(s)} \left(\sum_{i \in p} l(i) \right) \tag{1}$$

where $P(s)$ are possible parses of the sentence, and the *loss* (or cost) l of parse p is summed over the inferences i that lead to the parse. To find $\hat{p}$, the parsing algorithm considers a sequence of states. The initial state contains terminal items, whose labels are the POS tags given by Ratnaparkhi (1996). The parser considers a set of (bottom-up) inferences at each state. Each inference results in a successor state to be placed on the agenda. The loss function l can consider arbitrary properties of the input and parse state,[2] which precludes a tractable dynamic programming solution to Equation 1. Therefore, we do standard agenda-based parsing, but instead of items our agenda stores entire states, as per more general best-first search over parsing hypergraphs (Klein & Manning, 2001). Each time we pop a state from the agenda, l computes a loss for the bottom-up inferences generated from that state. If the loss of the popped state exceeds that of the current best complete parse, search is done and we have found the optimal parse.

[2] I.e. we make no context-free assumptions.

3 Training Method

3.1 General Setting

From each training inference $i \in I$ we generate the tuple $\langle X(i), y(i), b(i) \rangle$. $X(i)$ is a feature vector describing i, with each element in $\{0, 1\}$. The observed y-value $y(i) \in \{-1, +1\}$ is determined by whether i is a correct inference or not. Some training examples might be more important than others, so each is given an initial bias $b(i) \in \mathbb{R}^+$.

Our goal during training is to induce a real-valued inference scoring function (hypothesis) $h(i; \alpha)$, which is a linear model parameterized by a vector α of reals:

$$h(i; \alpha) = \alpha \cdot X(i) = \sum_f \alpha_f \cdot X_f(i) \tag{2}$$

Each f is a feature. The sign of $h(i; \alpha)$ predicts the y-value of i and the magnitude gives the confidence in this prediction.

The training procedure optimizes α to minimize the expected risk R:

$$R(I; \alpha) = L(I; \alpha) + \Omega(\alpha) \tag{3}$$

In principle, L can be any loss function, but in the present work we use the log-loss (Collins et al., 2002):

$$L(I; \alpha) = \sum_{i \in I} l(i; \alpha) = \sum_{i \in I} b(i) \cdot \sigma(\mu(i; \alpha)) \tag{4}$$

where:

$$\sigma(\mu) = \ln(1 + \exp(-\mu)) \tag{5}$$

and the *margin* of inference i under the current model α is:

$$\mu(i; \alpha) = y(i) \cdot h(i; \alpha) \tag{6}$$

For a particular choice of α, $l(i)$ in Equation 1 is computed according to Equation 4 using $y(i) = +1$ and $b(i) = 1$.

$\Omega(\alpha)$ in Equation 3 is a regularizer, which penalizes overly complex models to reduce overfitting and generalization error. We use the ℓ_1 penalty:

$$\Omega(\alpha) = \sum_f \lambda \cdot |\alpha_f| \tag{7}$$

where λ is the ℓ_1 parameter that controls the strength of the regularizer. This choice of objective R is motivated by Ng (2004), who suggests that, given a learning setting where the number of irrelevant features is exponential in the number of training examples, we can nonetheless learn effectively by building decision trees to minimize the ℓ_1-regularized log-loss. Conversely, Ng (2004) suggests that most of the learning algorithms commonly used by discriminative parsers *will* overfit when exponentially many irrelevant features are present.[3]

Learning over an exponential feature space is the very setting we have in mind. *A priori*, we define only a set A of simple *atomic* features (see §4). However, the learner induces *compound* features, each of which is a conjunction of possibly negated atomic features. Each atomic feature can have three values (yes/no/don't care), so the size of the compound feature space is $3^{|A|}$, exponential in the number of atomic features. It was also exponential in the number of training examples in our experiments ($|A| \approx |I|$).

We use an ensemble of confidence-rated decision trees (Schapire & Singer, 1999) to represent h.[4] Each node in a decision tree corresponds to a compound feature, and the leaves of the decision trees keep track of the parameter values of the compound features they represent. To score an inference using a decision tree, we percolate the inference down to a leaf and return that leaf's confidence. The overall score given to an inference by the whole ensemble is the sum of the confidences returned by the trees in the ensemble.

3.2 Boosting ℓ_1-Regularized Decision Trees

Listing 1 presents our training algorithm. (Sampling will be explained in §3.3. Until then, assume that the sample S is the entire training set I.) At the beginning of training, the ensemble is empty, $\alpha = \mathbf{0}$, and the ℓ_1 parameter λ is set to ∞. We train until the objective cannot be further reduced for the current choice of λ. We then relax the regularization penalty by decreasing λ and continuing training. We also determine the accuracy of the parser on a held-out development set using the previous λ value (before it was decreased), and can stop training when this accuracy plateaus. In this way, instead of choosing the best λ heuristically, we can optimize it during a single training run (Turian & Melamed, 2005).

Listing 1 Training algorithm.

procedure TRAIN(I)
    ensemble $\leftarrow \emptyset$
    $h(i) \leftarrow 0$ for all $i \in I$
    for $T = 1 \ldots \infty$ **do**
        $S \leftarrow$ priority sample I
        extract $X(i)$ for all $i \in S$
        build decision tree t using S
        percolate every $i \in I$ to a leaf node in t
        for each leaf f in t **do**
            choose α_f to minimize R
            add α_f to $h(i)$ for all i in this leaf

Our strategy for optimizing α to minimize the objective R (Equation 3) is a variant of steepest descent (Perkins et al., 2003). Each training iteration has several steps. First, we choose some new compound features that have high magnitude gradient with respect to the objective function. We do this by building a new decision tree, whose leaves represent the new compound features.[5] Second, we confidence-rate each leaf to minimize the objective over the examples that percolate down to that leaf. Finally, we append the decision tree to the ensemble and update parameter vector α accordingly. In this manner, compound feature selection is performed incrementally *during* training, as opposed to *a priori*.

To build each decision tree, we begin with a root node, and we recursively split nodes by choosing a splitting feature that will allow us to decrease the objective. We have:

$$\frac{\partial L(I;\alpha)}{\partial \alpha_f} = \sum_{i \in I} \frac{\partial l(i;\alpha)}{\partial \mu(i;\alpha)} \cdot \frac{\partial \mu(i;\alpha)}{\partial \alpha_f} \tag{8}$$

where:

$$\frac{\partial \mu(i;\alpha)}{\partial \alpha_f} = y(i) \cdot X_f(i) \tag{9}$$

We define the *weight* of an example under the current model as:

$$w(i;\alpha) = -\frac{\partial l(i;\alpha)}{\partial \mu(i;\alpha)} = b(i) \cdot \frac{1}{1 + \exp(\mu(i;\alpha))}. \tag{10}$$

[3]including the following learning algorithms:
- unregularized logistic regression
- logistic regression with an ℓ_2 penalty (i.e. a Gaussian prior)
- SVMs using most kernels
- multilayer neural nets trained by backpropagation
- the perceptron algorithm

[4]Turian and Melamed (2005) show that that decision trees applied to parsing have higher accuracy and training speed than decision stumps.

[5]Any given compound feature can appear in more than one tree.

and:

$$W_f^{\bar{y}}(I;\alpha) = \sum_{\substack{i \in I \\ X_f(i)=1, y(i)=\bar{y}}} w(i;\alpha) \tag{11}$$

Combining Equations 8–11 gives:[6]

$$\frac{\partial L}{\partial \alpha_f} = W_f^{-1} - W_f^{+1} \tag{12}$$

We define the *gain* G_f of feature f as:

$$G_f = \max\left(0, \left|\frac{\partial L}{\partial \alpha_f}\right| - \lambda\right) \tag{13}$$

Equation 13 has this form because the gradient of the penalty term is undefined at $\alpha_f = 0$. This discontinuity is why ℓ_1 regularization tends to produce sparse models. If $G_f = 0$, then the objective R is at its minimum with respect to parameter α_f. Otherwise, G_f is the magnitude of the gradient of the objective as we adjust α_f in the appropriate direction.

The gain of splitting node f using some atomic feature a is defined as

$$\check{G}_f(a) = G_{f \wedge a} + G_{f \wedge \neg a} \tag{14}$$

We allow node f to be split only by atomic features a that increase the gain, i.e. $\check{G}_f(a) > G_f$. If no such feature exists, then f becomes a leaf node of the decision tree and α_f becomes one of the values to be optimized during the parameter update step. Otherwise, we choose atomic feature $\hat{a}$ to split node f:

$$\hat{a} = \arg\max_{a \in A} \check{G}_f(a) \tag{15}$$

This split creates child nodes $f \wedge \hat{a}$ and $f \wedge \neg\hat{a}$. If no root node split has positive gain, then training has converged for the current choice of ℓ_1 parameter λ.

Parameter update is done sequentially on only the most recently added compound features, which correspond to the leaves of the new decision tree. After the entire tree is built, we percolate examples down to their appropriate leaf nodes. We then choose for each leaf node f the parameter α_f that minimizes the objective R over the examples in that leaf. Decision trees ensure that these compound features are mutually exclusive, so they can be directly optimized independently of each other using a line search over the objective R.

[6] Since α is fixed during a particular training iteration and I is fixed throughout training, we omit parameters $(I;\alpha)$ henceforth.

3.3 Sampling for Faster Feature Selection

Building a decision tree using the entire example set I can be very expensive, which we will demonstrate in §4.2. However, feature selection can be effective even if we don't examine every example. Since the weight of high-margin examples can be several orders of magnitude lower than that of low-margin examples (Equation 10), the contribution of the high-margin examples to feature weights (Equation 11) will be insignificant. Therefore, we can ignore most examples during feature selection as long as we have good estimates of feature weights, which in turn give good estimates of the loss gradients (Equation 12).

As shown in Step 1.5 of Listing 1, before building each decision tree we use priority sampling (Duffield et al., 2005) to choose a small subset of the examples according to the example weights given by the current classifier, and the tree is built using only this subset. We make the sample small enough that its entire atomic feature matrix will fit in memory. To optimize decision tree building, we compute and cache the sample's atomic feature matrix in advance (Step 1.6).

Even if the sample is missing important information in one iteration, the training procedure is capable of recovering it from samples used in subsequent iterations. Moreover, even if a sample's gain estimates are inaccurate and the feature selection step chooses irrelevant compound features, confidence updates are based upon the entire training set and the regularization penalty will prevent irrelevant features from having their parameters move away from zero.

3.4 The Training Set

Our training set I contains all inferences considered in every state along the correct path for each gold-standard parse tree (Sagae & Lavie, 2005).[7] This method of generating training examples does not require a working parser and can be run prior to any training. The downside of this approach is that it minimizes the error of the parser at *correct* states only. It does not account for compounded error or teach the parser to recover from mistakes gracefully.

[7] Since parsing is done deterministically right-to-left, there can be no more than one correct inference at each state.

Turian and Melamed (2005) observed that uniform example biases $b(i)$ produced lower accuracy as training progressed, because the induced classifiers minimized the *example-wise* error. Since we aim to minimize the state-wise error, we express this bias by assigning every training *state* equal value, and—for the examples generated from that state—sharing half the value uniformly among the negative examples and the other half uniformly among the positive examples.

Although there are $O(n^2)$ possible spans over a frontier containing n items, we reduce this to the $O(n)$ inferences that cannot have more than 5 children. With no restriction on the number of children, there would be $O(n^2)$ bottom-up inferences at each state. However, only 0.57% of non-terminals in the preprocessed development set have more than five children.

Like Turian and Melamed (2005), we parallelize training by inducing 26 label classifiers (one for each non-terminal label in the Penn Treebank). Parallelization might not uniformly reduce training time because different label classifiers train at different rates. However, parallelization uniformly reduces *memory* usage because each label classifier trains only on inferences whose consequent item has that label. Even after parallelization, the atomic feature matrix cannot be cached in memory. We can store the training inferences in memory using only an *indirect* representation. More specifically, for each inference i in the training set, we cache in memory several values: a pointer i to a tree cut, its y-value $y(i)$, its bias $b(i)$, and its confidence $h(i)$ under the current model. We cache $h(i)$ throughout training because it is needed both in computing the gradient of the objective during decision tree building (Step 1.7) as well as subsequent minimization of the objective over the decision tree leaves (Step 1.10). We update the confidences at the end of each training iteration using the newly added tree (Step 1.11).

The most costly operation during training is to access the feature values in $X(i)$. An atomic feature *test* determines the value $X_a(i)$ for a single atomic feature a by examining the tree cut pointed to by inference i. Alternately, we can perform atomic feature *extraction*, i.e. determine *all* non-zero atomic features over i.[8] Extraction is 100–1000 times more expensive than a single test, but is necessary during decision tree building (Step 1.7) because we need the entire vector $X(i)$ to accumulate inferences in children nodes. Essentially, for each inference i that falls in some node f, we accumulate $w(i)$ in $W^{y(i)}_{f \wedge a}$ for all a with $X_a(i) = 1$. After all the inferences in a node have been accumulated, we try to split the node (Equation 15). The negative child weights are each determined as $W^y_{f \wedge \neg a} = W^y_f - W^y_{f \wedge a}$.

4 Experiments

We follow Taskar et al. (2004) and Turian and Melamed (2005) in training and testing on $\leq$ 15 word sentences in the English Penn Treebank (Taylor et al., 2003). We used sections 02–21 for training, section 22 for development, and section 23, for testing. We use the same preprocessing steps as Turian and Melamed (2005): during both training and testing, the parser is given text POS-tagged by the tagger of Ratnaparkhi (1996), with capitalization stripped and outermost punctuation removed.

For reasons given in Turian and Melamed (2006), items are inferred bottom-up right-to-left. As mentioned in §2, the parser cannot infer any item that crosses an item already in the state. To ensure the parser does not enter an infinite loop, no two items in a state can have both the same span and the same label. Given these restrictions, there were roughly 40 million training examples. These were partitioned among the constituent label classifiers.

Our atomic feature set A contains features of the form "is there an item in group J whose label/headword/headtag/headtagclass[9] is 'X'?". Possible values of 'X' for each predicate are collected from the training data. Some examples of possible values for J include the last n child items, the first n left context items, all right context items, and the terminal items dominated by the non-head child items. Space constraints prevent enumeration of the headtagclasses and atomic feature templates, which are

[8]Extraction need not take the naïve approach of performing $|A|$ different tests, and can be optimized by using knowledge about the nature of the atomic feature templates.

[9]The predicate headtagclass is a supertype of the headtag. Given our compound features, these are not strictly necessary, but they accelerate training. An example is "proper noun," which contains the POS tags given to singular and plural proper nouns.

Figure 1 F_1 score of our parser on the development set of the Penn Treebank, using only $\leq$ 15 word sentences. The dashed line indicates the percent of NP example weight lost due to sampling. The bottom x-axis shows the number of non-zero parameters in each parser, summed over all label classifiers.

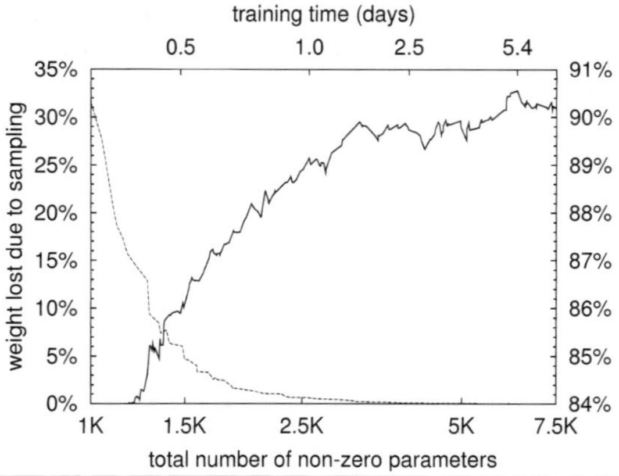

instead provided at the URL given in the abstract. These templates gave 1.1 million different atomic features. We experimented with smaller feature sets, but found that accuracy was lower. Charniak and Johnson (2005) use linguistically more sophisticated features, and Bod (2003) and Kudo et al. (2005) use sub-tree features, all of which we plan to try in future work.

We evaluated our parser using the standard PARSEVAL measures (Black et al., 1991): labelled precision, labelled recall, and labelled F-measure (Prec., Rec., and F_1, respectively), which are based on the number of non-terminal items in the parser's output that match those in the gold-standard parse. The solid curve Figure 1 shows the accuracy of the parser over the development set as training progressed. The parser exceeded 89% F-measure after 2.5 days of training. The peak F-measure was 90.55%, achieved at 5.4 days using 6.3K active parameters. We omit details given by Turian and Melamed (2006) in favor of a longer discussion in §4.2.

4.1 Test Set Results

To situate our results in the literature, we compare our results to those reported by Taskar et al. (2004) and Turian and Melamed (2005) for their discriminative parsers, which were also trained and tested on $\leq$ 15 word sentences. We also compare our parser to a representative non-discriminative parser (Bikel, 2004),[10] the only one that we were able to train and test under exactly the same experimental conditions (including the use of POS tags from Ratnaparkhi (1996)). Table 1 shows the PARSEVAL results of these four parsers on the test set.

Table 1 PARSEVAL results of parsers on the test set, using only $\leq$ 15 word sentences.

	F_1 %	Rec. %	Prec. %
Turian and Melamed (2005)	87.13	86.47	87.80
Bikel (2004)	88.30	87.85	88.75
Taskar et al. (2004)	89.12	89.10	89.14
our parser	89.40	89.26	89.55

Table 2 Profile of an NP training iteration, given in seconds, using an AMD Opteron 242 (64-bit, 1.6Ghz). Steps refer to Listing 1.

Step	Description	mean	stddev	%
1.5	Sample	1.5s	0.07s	0.7%
1.6	Extraction	38.2s	0.13s	18.6%
1.7	Build tree	127.6s	27.60s	62.3%
1.8	Percolation	31.4s	4.91s	15.3%
1.9–11	Leaf updates	6.2s	1.75s	3.0%
1.5–11	Total	204.9s	32.6s	100.0%

4.2 Efficiency

40% of non-terminals in the Penn Treebank are NPs. Consequently, the bottleneck in training is induction of the NP classifier. It was trained on 1.65 million examples. Each example had an average of 440 non-zero atomic features (stddev 123), so the *direct* representation of each example requires a minimum $440 \cdot \text{sizeof(int)} = 1760$ bytes, and the entire atomic feature matrix would require 1760 bytes $\cdot$ 1.65 million = 2.8 GB. Conversely, an indirectly represent inference requires no more 32 bytes: two floats (the cached confidence $h(i)$ and the bias term $b(i)$), a pointer to a tree cut (i), and a bool (the y-value $y(i)$). Indirectly storing the entire example set requires only 32 bytes $\cdot$ 1.65 million = 53 MB plus the treebank and tree cuts, a total of 400 MB in our implementation.

We used a sample size of $|S| = 100,000$ examples to build each decision tree, 16.5 times fewer than the entire example set. The dashed curve in Figure 1

[10]Bikel (2004) is a "clean room" reimplementation of the Collins (1999) model with comparable accuracy.

shows the percent of NP example weight lost due to sampling. As training progresses, fewer examples are informative to the model. Even though we ignore 94% of examples during feature selection, sampling loses less than 1% of the example weight after a day of training.

The NP classifier used in our final parser was an ensemble containing 2316 trees, which took five days to build. Overall, there were 96871 decision tree leaves, only 2339 of which were non-zero. There were an average of 40.4 (7.4 stddev) decision tree splits between the root of a tree and a non-zero leaf, and nearly all non-zero leaves were conjunctions of atomic feature *negations* (e.g. ¬(some child item is a verb) ∧ ¬(some child item is a preposition)). The non-zero leaf confidences were quite small in magnitude (0.107 mean, 0.069 stddev) but the training example margins over the entire ensemble were nonetheless quite high: 11.7 mean (2.92 stddev) for correct inferences, 30.6 mean (11.2 stddev) for incorrect inferences.

Table 2 profiles an NP training iteration, in which one decision tree is created and added to the NP ensemble. Feature selection in our algorithm (Steps 1.5–1.7) takes $1.5+38.2+127.6 = 167.3$s, far faster than in naïve approaches. If we didn't do sampling but had 2.8GB to spare, we could eliminate the extraction step (Step 1.6) and instead cache the entire atomic feature matrix before the loop. However, tree building (Step 1.7) scales linearly in the number of examples, and would take $16.5 \cdot 127.6\text{s} = 2105.4\text{s}$ using the entire example set. If we didn't do sampling and couldn't cache the atomic feature matrix, tree building would also require repeatedly performing extraction. The number of individual feature extractions needed to build a single decision tree is the sum over the internal nodes of the number of examples that percolate down to that node. There are an average of 40.8 (7.8 stddev) internal nodes in each tree and most of the examples fall in nearly all of them. This property is caused by the lopsided trees induced under ℓ_1 regularization. A conservative estimate is that each decision tree requires 25 extractions times the number of examples. So extraction would add at least $25 \cdot 16.5 \cdot 38.2\text{s} = 15757.5s$ on top of 2105.40s, and hence building each decision tree would take at least $(15757.5+2105.40)/167.3 \approx$ *100 times* as long as it does currently.

Our decision tree ensembles contain over two orders of magnitude more compound features than those in Turian and Melamed (2005). Our overall training time was roughly equivalent to theirs. This ratio corroborates the above estimate.

5 Discussion

The NP classifier was trained only on the 1.65 million NP examples in the 9753 training sentences with ≤ 15 words (168.8 examples/sentence). The number of examples generated is quadratic in the sentence length, so there are 41.7 million NP examples in all 39832 training sentences of the whole Penn Treebank (1050 examples/sentence), 25 times as many as we are currently using.

The time complexity of each step in the training loop (Steps 1.5–11) is linear over the number of examples used by that step. When we scale up to the full treebank, feature selection will not require a sample 25 times larger, so it will no longer be the bottleneck in training. Instead, each iteration will be dominated by choosing leaf confidences and then updating the cached example confidences, which would require $25 \cdot (31.4\text{s} + 6.2\text{s}) = 940\text{s}$ per iteration. These steps are crucial to the current training algorithm, because it is important to have example confidences that are current with respect to the model. Otherwise, we cannot determine the examples most poorly classified by the current model, and will have no basis for choosing an informative sample.

We might try to save training time by building *many* decision trees over a single sample and then updating the confidences of the entire example set using all the new trees. But, if this confidence update is done using feature tests, then we have merely deferred the cost of the confidence update over the entire example set. The amount of training done on a particular sample is proportional to the time subsequently spent updating confidences over the entire example set. To spend less time doing confidence updates, we must use a training regime that is *sub*-linear with respect to the training time. For example, Riezler (2004) reports that the ℓ_1 regularization term drives many of the model's parameters to zero during conjugate gradient optimization, which are then pruned before subsequent optimization steps to avoid numerical instability. Instead of building decision tree(s) at each iteration, we could perform n-best feature selection followed by parallel optimization of the objective over the sample.

The main limitation of our work so far is that we can do training reasonably quickly only on short sentences, because a sentence with n words generates $O(n^2)$ training inferences in total. Although generating training examples in advance without a working parser (Sagae & Lavie, 2005) is much faster than using inference (Collins & Roark, 2004; Henderson, 2004; Taskar et al., 2004), our training time can probably be decreased further by choosing a parsing strategy with a lower branching factor. Like our work, Ratnaparkhi (1999) and Sagae and Lavie (2005) generate examples off-line, but their parsing strategies are essentially shift-reduce so each sentence generates only $O(n)$ training examples.

6 Conclusion

Our work has made advances in both accuracy and training speed of discriminative parsing. As far as we know, we present the first discriminative parser that surpasses a generative baseline on constituent parsing without using a generative component, and it does so with minimal linguistic cleverness.

The main bottleneck in our setting was memory. We could store the examples in memory only using an indirect representation. The most costly operation during training was accessing the features of a particular example from this indirect representation. We showed how to train a parser effectively under these conditions. In particular, we used principled sampling to estimate loss gradients and reduce the number of feature extractions. This approximation increased the speed of feature selection 100-fold.

We are exploring methods for scaling training up to larger example sets. We are also investigating the relationship between sample size, training time, classifier complexity, and accuracy. In addition, we shall make some standard improvements to our parser. Our parser should infer its own POS tags. A shift-reduce parsing strategy will generate fewer examples, and might lead to shorter training time. Lastly, we plan to give the model linguistically more sophisticated features. We also hope to apply the model to other structured learning tasks, such as syntax-driven SMT.

References

Bikel, D. M. (2004). Intricacies of Collins' parsing model. *Computational Linguistics*.

Black, E., Abney, S., Flickenger, D., Gdaniec, C., Grishman, R., Harrison, P., et al. (1991). A procedure for quantitatively comparing the syntactic coverage of English grammars. In *Speech and Natural Language*.

Bod, R. (2003). An efficient implementation of a new DOP model. In *EACL*.

Charniak, E., & Johnson, M. (2005). Coarse-to-fine n-best parsing and MaxEnt discriminative reranking. In *ACL*.

Collins, M. (1999). *Head-driven statistical models for natural language parsing*. Doctoral dissertation.

Collins, M., & Roark, B. (2004). Incremental parsing with the perceptron algorithm. In *ACL*.

Collins, M., Schapire, R. E., & Singer, Y. (2002). Logistic regression, AdaBoost and Bregman distances. *Machine Learning*, *48*(1-3).

Duffield, N., Lund, C., & Thorup, M. (2005). *Priority sampling estimating arbitrary subset sums*. (`http://arxiv.org/abs/cs.DS/0509026`)

Henderson, J. (2004). Discriminative training of a neural network statistical parser. In *ACL*.

Klein, D., & Manning, C. D. (2001). Parsing and hypergraphs. In *IWPT*.

Kudo, T., Suzuki, J., & Isozaki, H. (2005). Boosting-based parse reranking with subtree features. In *ACL*.

Ng, A. Y. (2004). Feature selection, ℓ_1 vs. ℓ_2 regularization, and rotational invariance. In *ICML*.

Perkins, S., Lacker, K., & Theiler, J. (2003). Grafting: Fast, incremental feature selection by gradient descent in function space. *Journal of Machine Learning Research*, *3*.

Ratnaparkhi, A. (1996). A maximum entropy part-of-speech tagger. In *EMNLP*.

Ratnaparkhi, A. (1999). Learning to parse natural language with maximum entropy models. *Machine Learning*, *34*(1-3).

Riezler, S. (2004). Incremental feature selection of ℓ_1 regularization for relaxed maximum-entropy modeling. In *EMNLP*.

Sagae, K., & Lavie, A. (2005). A classifier-based parser with linear run-time complexity. In *IWPT*.

Schapire, R. E., & Singer, Y. (1999). Improved boosting using confidence-rated predictions. *Machine Learning*, *37*(3).

Smith, N. A., & Eisner, J. (2005). Contrastive estimation: Training log-linear models on unlabeled data. In *ACL*.

Taskar, B., Klein, D., Collins, M., Koller, D., & Manning, C. (2004). Max-margin parsing. In *EMNLP*.

Taylor, A., Marcus, M., & Santorini, B. (2003). The Penn Treebank: an overview. In A. Abeillé (Ed.), *Treebanks: Building and using parsed corpora* (chap. 1).

Turian, J., & Melamed, I. D. (2005). Constituent parsing by classification. In *IWPT*.

Turian, J., & Melamed, I. D. (2006). Advances in discriminative parsing. In *ACL*.

All-word prediction as the ultimate confusable disambiguation

Antal van den Bosch
ILK / Dept. of Language and Information Science, Tilburg University
P.O. Box 90153, NL-5000 LE Tilburg, The Netherlands
Antal.vdnBosch@uvt.nl

Abstract

We present a classification-based word prediction model based on IGTREE, a decision-tree induction algorithm with favorable scaling abilities and a functional equivalence to n-gram models with back-off smoothing. Through a first series of experiments, in which we train on Reuters newswire text and test either on the same type of data or on general or fictional text, we demonstrate that the system exhibits log-linear increases in prediction accuracy with increasing numbers of training examples. Trained on 30 million words of newswire text, prediction accuracies range between 12.6% on fictional text and 42.2% on newswire text. In a second series of experiments we compare all-words prediction with confusable prediction, i.e., the same task, but specialized to predicting among limited sets of words. Confusable prediction yields high accuracies on nine example confusable sets in all genres of text. The confusable approach outperforms the all-words-prediction approach, but with more data the difference decreases.

1 Introduction

Word prediction is an intriguing language engineering semi-product. Arguably it is the "archetypical prediction problem in natural language processing" (Even-Zohar and Roth, 2000). It is usually not an engineering end in itself to predict the next word in a sequence, or fill in a blanked-out word in a sequence. Yet, it could be an asset in higher-level proofing or authoring tools, e.g. to be able to automatically discern among confusables and thereby to detect confusable errors (Golding and Roth, 1999; Even-Zohar and Roth, 2000; Banko and Brill, 2001; Huang and Powers, 2001). It could alleviate problems with low-frequency and unknown words in natural language processing and information retrieval, by replacing them with likely and higher-frequency alternatives that carry similar information. And also, since the task of word prediction is a direct interpretation of language modeling, a word prediction system could provide useful information for to be used in speech recognition systems.

A unique aspect of the word prediction task, as compared to most other tasks in natural language processing, is that real-world examples abound in large amounts. Any digitized text can be used as training material for a word prediction system capable of learning from examples, and nowadays gigascale and terascale document collections are available for research purposes.

A specific type of word prediction is confusable prediction, i.e., learn to predict among limited sets of confusable words such as *to/two/too* and *there/their/they're* (Golding and Roth, 1999; Banko and Brill, 2001). Having trained a confusable predictor on occurrences of words within a confusable set, it can be applied to any new occurrence of a word from the set; if its prediction based on the context deviates from the word actually present, then

Workshop on Computationally Hard Problemsand Joint Inference in Speech and Language Processing, pages 25–32,
New York City, New York, June 2006.

this word might be a confusable error, and the classifier's prediction might be its correction. Confusable prediction and correction is a strong asset in proofing tools.

In this paper we generalize the word prediction task to predicting *any* word in context. This is basically the task of a generic language model. An explicit choice for the particular study on "all-words" prediction is to encode context only by words, and not by any higher-level linguistic non-terminals which have been investigated in related work on word prediction (Wu et al., 1999; Even-Zohar and Roth, 2000). This choice leaves open the question how the same tasks can be learned from examples when non-terminal symbols are taken into account as well.

The choice for our algorithm, a decision-tree approximation of k-nearest-neigbor (k-NN) based or memory-based learning, is motivated by the fact that, as we describe later in this paper, this particular algorithm can scale up to predicting tens of thousands of words, while simultaneously being able to scale up to tens of millions of examples as training material, predicting words at useful rates of hundreds to thousands of words per second. Another motivation for our choice is that our decision-tree approximation of k-nearest neighbor classification is functionally equivalent to back-off smoothing (Zavrel and Daelemans, 1997); not only does it share its performance capacities with n-gram models with back-off smoothing, it also shares its scaling abilities with these models, while being able to handle large values of n.

The article is structured as follows. In Section 2 we describe what data we selected for our experiments, and we provide an overview of the experimental methodology used throughout the experiments, including a description of the IGTREE algorithm central to our study. In Section 3 the results of the word prediction experiments are presented, and the subsequent Section 4 contains the experimental results of the experiments on confusables. We briefly relate our work to earlier work that inspired the current study in Section 5. The results are discussed, and conclusions are drawn in Section 6.

2 Data preparation and experimental setup

First, we identify the textual corpora used. We then describe the general experimental setup of learning curve experiments, and the IGTREE decision-tree induction algorithm used throughout all experiments.

2.1 Data

To generate our word prediction examples, we used the "Reuters Corpus Volume 1 (English Language, 1996-08-20 to 1997-08-19)"[1]. We tokenized this corpus with a rule-based tokenizer, and used all 130,396,703 word and punctuation tokens for experimentation. In the remainder of the article we make no difference between words and punctuation markers; both are regarded as tokens. We separated the final 100,000 tokens as a held-out test set, henceforth referred to as REUTERS, and kept the rest as training set, henceforth TRAIN-REUTERS.

Additionally, we selected two test sets taken from different corpora. First, we used the Project Gutenberg[2] version of the novel *Alice's Adventures in Wonderland* by Lewis Carroll (Carroll, 1865), henceforth ALICE. As the third test set we selected all tokens of the Brown corpus part of the Penn Treebank (Marcus et al., 1993), a selected portion of the original one-million word Brown corpus (Kučera and Francis, 1967), a collection of samples of American English in many different genres, from sources printed in 1961; we refer to this test set as BROWN. In sum, we have three test sets, covering texts from the same genre and source as the training data, a fictional novel, and a mix of genres wider than the training set.

Table 1 summarizes the key training and test set statistics. As the table shows, the cross-domain coverages for unigrams and bigrams are rather low; not only are these numbers the best-case performance ceilings, they also imply that a lot of contextual information used by the machine learning method used in this paper will be partly unknown to the learner, especially in texts from other domains than the training set.

[1] For availability of the Reuters corpus, see http://about.reuters.com/researchandstandards/corpu

[2] Project Gutenberg: http://www.gutenberg.net.

Data set	Genre	# Tokens	Coverage (%)	
TRAIN-REUTERS	news	30 million	unigram	bigram
REUTERS	news	100,000	91.0	83.6
ALICE	fiction	33,361	85.2	70.1
BROWN	mixed	453,446	75.9	72.3

Table 1: Training and test set sources, genres, sizes in terms of numbers of tokens, and unigram and bigram coverage (%) of the training set on the test sets.

2.2 Experimental setup

All experiments described in this article take the form of learning curve experiments (Banko and Brill, 2001), in which a sequence of training sets is generated with increasing size, where each size training set is used to train a model for word prediction, which is subsequently tested on a held-out test set – which is fixed throughout the whole learning curve experiment. Training set sizes are exponentially grown, as earlier studies have shown that at a linear scale, performance effects tend to decrease in size, but that when measured with exponentially growing training sets, near-constant (i.e. log-linear) improvements are observed (Banko and Brill, 2001).

We create incrementally-sized training sets for the word prediction task on the basis of the TRAIN-REUTERS set. Each training subset is created backward from the point at which the final 100,000-word REUTERS set starts. The increments are exponential with base number 10, and for every power of 10 we cut off training sets at n times that power, where $n = 1, 2, 3, \ldots, 8, 9$ (for example, $10, 20, \ldots, 80, 90$).

The actual examples to learn from are created by *windowing* over all sequences of tokens. We encode examples by taking a left context window spanning seven tokens, and a right context also spanning seven tokens. Thus, the task is represented by a growing number of examples, each characterized by 14 positional features carrying tokens as values, and one class label representing the word to be predicted. The choice for 14 is intended to cover at least the superficially most important positional features. We assume that a word more distant than seven positions left or right of a focus word will almost never be more informative for the task than any of the words within this scope.

2.3 IGTree

IGTree (Daelemans et al., 1997) is an algorithm for the top-down induction of decision trees. It compresses a database of labeled examples into a lossless-compression decision-tree structure that preserves the labeling information of all examples, and technically should be named a *trie* according to (Knuth, 1973). A labeled example is a feature-value vector, where features in our study represent a sequence of tokens representing context, associated with a symbolic class label representing the word to be predicted. An IGTREE is composed of nodes that each represent a partition of the original example database, and are labeled by the most frequent class of that partition. The root node of the trie thus represents the entire example database and carries the most frequent value as class label, while end nodes (leafs) represent a *homogeneous* partition of the database in which all examples have the same class label. A node is either a leaf, or is a non-ending node that branches out to nodes at a deeper level of the trie. Each branch represents a test on a feature value; branches fanning out of one node test on values of the same feature.

To attain high compression levels, IGTREE adopts the same heuristic that most other decision-tree induction algorithms adopt, such as C4.5 (Quinlan, 1993), which is to always branch out testing on the most informative, or most class-discriminative features first. Like C4.5, IGTREE uses information gain (IG) to estimate the most informative features. The IG of feature i is measured by computing the difference in uncertainty (i.e. entropy) between the situations without and with knowledge of the value of that feature with respect to predicting the class label: $IG_i = H(C) - \sum_{v \in V_i} P(v) \times H(C|v)$, where C is the set of class labels, V_i is the set of values for feature i, and $H(C) = -\sum_{c \in C} P(c) \log_2 P(c)$ is the entropy of the class labels. In contrast with C4.5, IGTREE computes the IG of all features once on the full database of training examples, makes a feature ordering once on these computed IG values, and uses this ordering throughout the whole trie.

Another difference with C4.5 is that IGTREE does not prune its produced trie, so that it performs a lossless compression of the labeling information of the original example database. As long as the database does not contain fully ambiguous examples (with the same features, but different class labels), the trie produced by IGTREE is able to reproduce the classifications of all examples in the original example database perfectly.

Due to the fact that IGTREE computes the IG of all features once, it is functionally equivalent to IB1-IG (Daelemans et al., 1999), a k-nearest neighbor classifier for symbolic features, with $k = 1$ and using a particular feature weighting in the similarity function in which the weight of each feature is larger than the sum of all weights of features with a lower weight (e.g. as in the exponential sequence $1, 2, 4, 8, \ldots$ where $2 > 1$, $4 > (1 + 2)$, $8 > (1 + 2 + 4)$, etc.). Both algorithms will base their classification on the example that matches on most features, ordered by their IG, and guess a majority class of the set of examples represented at the level of mismatching. IGTREE, therefore, can be seen as an approximation of IB1-IG with $k = 1$ that has favorable asymptotic complexities as compared to IB1-IG.

IGTREE's computational bottleneck is the trie construction process, which has an asymptotic complexity of $O(n\ lg(v)\ f)$ of CPU, where n is the number of training examples, v is the average branching factor of IGTREE (how many branches fan out of a node, on average), and f is the number of features. Storing the trie, on the other hand, costs $O(n)$ in memory, which is less than the $O(n\ f)$ of IB1-IG. Classification in IGTREE takes an efficient $O(f\ lg(v))$ of CPU, versus the cumbersome worst-case $O(n\ f)$ of IB1-IG, that is, in the typical case that n is much higher than f or v.

Interestingly, IGTREE is functionally equivalent to back-off smoothing (Zavrel and Daelemans, 1997), with the IG of the features determining the order in which to back off, which in the case of word prediction tends to be from the outer context to the inner context of the immediately neighboring words. Like with probabilistic n-gram based models with a back-off smoothing scheme, IGTREE will prefer matches that are as exact as possible (e.g. matching on all 14 features), but will back-off by disregarding lesser important features first, down to a simple bigram model drawing on the most important feature, the immediately preceding left word. In sum, IGTREE shares its scaling abilities with n-gram models, and its implementation allows it to handle large values of n.

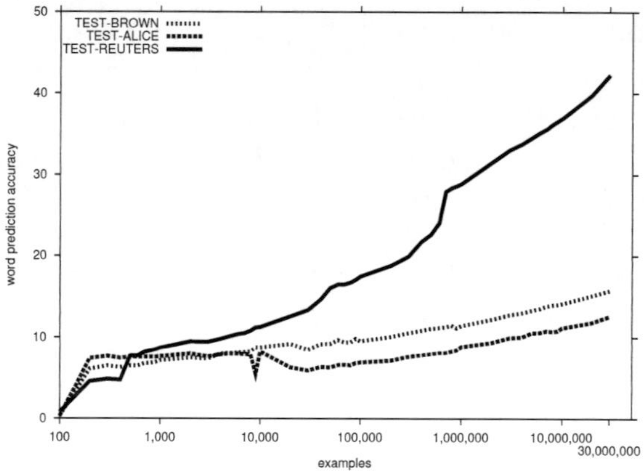

Figure 1: Learning curves of word prediction accuracies of IGTREE trained on TRAIN-REUTERS, and tested on REUTERS, ALICE, and BROWN.

3 All-words prediction

3.1 Learning curve experiments

The word prediction accuracy learning curves computed on the three test sets, and trained on increasing portions of TRAIN-REUTERS, are displayed in Figure 1. The best accuracy observed is 42.2% with 30 million training examples, on REUTERS. Apparently, training and testing on the same type of data yields markedly higher prediction accuracies than testing on a different-type corpus. Accuracies on BROWN are slightly higher than on ALICE, but the difference is small; at 30 million training examples, the accuracy on ALICE is 12.6%, and on BROWN 15.8%.

A second observation is that all three learning curves are progressing upward with more training examples, and roughly at a constant log-linear rate. When estimating the rates after about 50,000 examples (before which the curves appear to be more volatile), with every tenfold increase of the number of training examples the prediction accuracy on REUTERS increases by a constant rate of about 8%, while the increases on ALICE and BROWN are both about 2% at every tenfold.

3.2 Memory requirements and classification speed

The numbers of nodes exhibit an interesting sublinear relation with respect to the number of training examples, which is in line with the asymptotic complexity order $O(n)$, where n is the number of training instances. An increasingly sublinear amount of nodes is necessary; while at 10,000 training instances the number of nodes is 7,759 (0.77 nodes per instance), at 1 million instances the number of nodes is 652,252 (0.65 nodes per instance), and at 30 million instances the number of nodes is 15,956,878 (0.53 nodes per instance).

A factor in classification speed is the average amount of branching. Conceivably, the word prediction task can lead to a large branching factor, especially in the higher levels of the tree. However, not every word can be the neighbor of every other word in finite amounts of text. To estimate the average branching factor of a tree we compute the fth root of the total number of nodes (f being the number of features, i.e. 14). The largest decision tree currently constructed is the one on the basis of a training set of 30 million examples, having 15,956,878 nodes. This tree has an average branching factor of $\sqrt[14]{15,956,878} \approx 3.27$; all other trees have smaller branching factors. Together with the fact that we have but 14 features, and the asymptotic complexity order of classification is $O(f\ lg(v))$, where v is the average branching factor, classification can be expected to be fast. Indeed, depending on the machine's CPU on which the experiment is run, we observe quite favorable classification speeds. Figure 2 displays the various speeds (in terms of the number of test tokens predicted per second) attained on the three test sets[3]. The best prediction accuracies are still attained at classification speeds of over a hundred predicted tokens per second. Two other relevant observations are that first, the classification speed hardly differs between the three test sets (BROWN is classified only slightly slower than the other two test sets), indicating that the classifier is spending a roughly comparable amount of searching through the decision trees regardless of genre differences. Second, the decrease in speed settles on a low log-linear rate after about one million examples. Thus, while trees grow linearly, and accuracy increases log-linearly, the speed of classification slowly diminishes at decreasing rates.

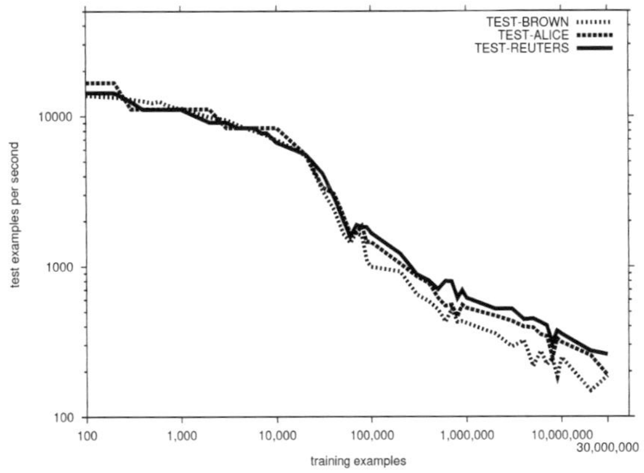

Figure 2: Word prediction speed, in terms of the number of classified test examples per second, measured on the three test sets, with increasing training examples. Both axes have a logarithmic scale.

4 Confusables

Word prediction from context can be considered a very hard task, due to the many choices open to the predictor at many points in the sequence. Predicting content words, for example, is often only possible through subtle contextual clues or by having the appropriate domain or world knowledge, or intimate knowledge of the writer's social context and intentions. In contrast, certain function words tend to be predictable due to the positions they take in syntactic phrase structure; their high frequency tends to ensure that plenty of examples of them in context are available.

Due to the important role of function words in syntactic structure, it can be quite disruptive for a parser and for human readers alike to encounter a mistyped function word that in its intended form is another function word. In fact, confusable errors between frequent forms occur relatively frequently. Examples of these so-called confusables in English are *there* versus *their* and the contraction *they're*; or the duo *than* and *then*. Confusables can arise from having the same pronunciation (homophones), or having very similar pronunciation (*country* or *county*) or spelling (*dessert*, *desert*), hav-

[3]Measurements were made on a GNU/Linux x86-based machine with 2.0 Ghz AMD Opteron processors.

ing very close lexical semantics (as between *among* and *between*), or being inflections or case variants of the same stem (*I* versus *me*, or *walk* versus *walks*), and may stem from a lack of concentration or experience by the writer.

Distinguishing between confusables is essentially the same task as word prediction, except that the number of alternative outcomes is small, e.g. two or three, rather than thousands or more. The typical application setting is also more specific: given that a writer has produced a text (e.g. a sentence in a word processor), it is possible to check the correctness of each occurrence of a word known to be part of a pair or triple of confusables.

We performed a series of experiments on disambiguating nine frequent confusables in English adopted from (Golding and Roth, 1999). We employed an experimental setting in which we use the same experimental data as before, in which only examples of the confusable words are drawn – note that we ignore possible confusable errors in both training and test set. This data set generation procedure reduces the amount of examples considerably. Despite having over 130 million words in TRAIN-REUTERS, frequent words such as *there* and *than* occur just over 100,000 times. To be able to run learning curves with more than this relatively small amount of examples, we expanded our training material with the New York Times of 1994 to 2002 (henceforth TRAIN-NYT), part of the English Gigaword collection published by the Linguistic Data Consortium, offering 1,096,950,281 tokens.

As a first illustration of the experimental outcomes, we focus on the three-way confusable *there – their – they're* for which we trained one classifier, which we henceforth refer to as a confusable expert. The learning curve results of this confusable expert are displayed in Figure 3 as the top three graphs. The logarithmic x-axis displays the full number of instances from TRAIN-REUTERS up to 130.3 million examples, and from TRAIN-NYT after this point. Counter to the learning curves in the all-words prediction experiments, and to the observation by (Banko and Brill, 2001), the learning curves of this confusable triple in the three different data sets flatten, and converge, remarkably, to a roughly similar score of about 98%. The convergence only occurs after examples from TRAIN-NYT are added.

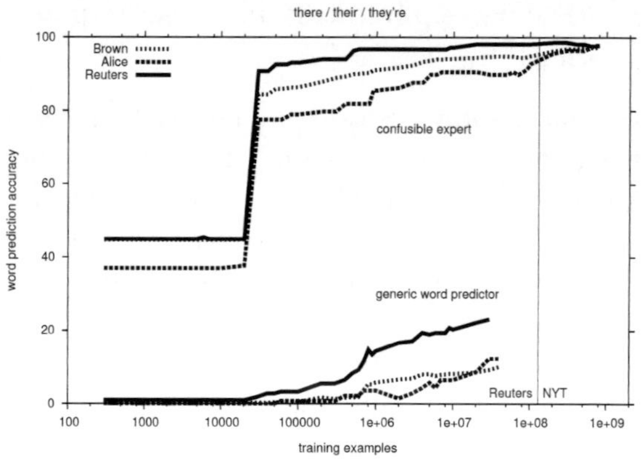

Figure 3: Learning curves in terms of word prediction accuracy on deciding between the confusable pair *there*, *their*, and *they're*, by IGTREE trained on TRAIN-REUTERS, and tested on REUTERS, ALICE, and BROWN. The top graphs are accuracies attained by the confusable expert; the bottom graphs are attained by the all-words predictor trained on TRAIN-REUTERS until 130 million examples, and on TRAIN-NYT beyond (marked by the vertical bar).

In the bottom of the same Figure 3 we have also plotted the word prediction accuracies on the three words *there*, *their*, and *they're* attained by the all-words predictor described in the previous section on the three test sets. The accuracies, or rather recall figures (i.e. the percentage of occurrences of the three words in the test sets which are correctly predicted as such), are considerably lower than those on the confusable disambiguation task.

Table 2 presents the experimental results obtained on nine confusable sets when training and testing on Reuters material. The third column lists the accuracy (or recall) scores of the all-words word prediction system at the maximal training set size of 30 million labeled examples. The fourth columns lists the accuracies attained by the confusable expert for the particular confusable pair or triple, measured at 30 million training examples, from which each particular confusable expert's examples are extracted. The amount of examples varies for the selected confusable sets, as can be seen in the second column.

Scores attained by the all-words predictor on these words vary from below 10% for relatively low-frequent words to around 60% for the more frequent confusables; the latter numbers are higher than the

Confusable set	Number of examples	Accuracy (%) by all-words prediction	confus. expert
cite - site - sight	2,286	0.0	100.0
accept - except	3,833	46.2	76.9
affect - effect	4,640	7.7	87.9
fewer - less	6,503	4.7	95.2
among - between	27,025	18.9	96.7
I - me	28,835	55.9	98.0
than - then	31,478	59.4	97.2
there - their - they're	58,081	23.1	96.8
to - too - two	553,453	60.6	93.4

Table 2: Disambiguation scores on nine confusable set, attained by the all-words prediction classifier trained on 30 million examples of TRAIN-REUTERS, and by confusable experts on the same training set. The second column displays the number of examples of each confusable set in the 30-million word training set; the list is ordered on this column.

Confusable set	Accuracy on test set (%) REUTERS	ALICE	BROWN
cite - site - sight	100.0	100.0	69.0
accept - except	84.6	100.0	97.0
affect - effect	92.3	100.0	89.5
fewer - less	90.5	100.0	97.2
among - between	94.4	77.8	74.4
I - me	99.0	98.3	98.3
than - then	97.2	92.9	95.8
there - their - they're	98.1	97.8	97.3
to - too - two	94.3	93.4	92.9

Table 3: Disambiguation scores on nine confusable set, attained by confusable experts trained on examples extracted from 1 billion words of text from TRAIN-REUTERS plus TRAIN-NYT, on the three test sets.

overall accuracy of this system on REUTERS. Nevertheless they are considerably lower than the scores attained by the confusable disambiguation classifiers, while being trained on many more examples (i.e., all 30 million available). Most of the confusable disambiguation classifiers attain accuracies of well above 90%.

When the learning curves are continued beyond TRAIN-REUTERS into TRAIN-NYT, about a thousand times as many training examples can be gathered as training data for the confusable experts. Table 3 displays the nine confusable expert's scores after being trained on examples extracted from a total of one billion words of text, measured on all three test sets. Apart from a few outliers, most scores are above 90%, and more importantly, the scores on ALICE and BROWN do not seriously lag behind those on REUTERS; some are even better.

5 Related work

As remarked in the cases reported in the literature directly related to the current article, word prediction is a core task to natural language processing, and one of the few that takes no annotation layer to provide data for supervised machine learning and probabilistic modeling (Golding and Roth, 1999; Even-Zohar and Roth, 2000; Banko and Brill, 2001). Our discrete, classificatio-nased approach has the same goal as probabilistic methods for language modeling for automatic speech recognition (Jelinek, 1998), and is also functionally equivalent to n-gram models with back-off smoothing (Zavrel and Daelemans, 1997).

The papers by Golding and Roth, and Banko and Brill on confusable correction focus on the more common type of *than/then* confusion that occurs a lot in the process of text production. Both pairs of authors use the confusable correction task to illustrate scaling issues, as we have. Golding and Roth illustrate that multiplicative weight-updating algorithms such as Winnow can deal with immense input feature spaces, where for each single classification only a small number of features is actually relevant (Golding and Roth, 1999). With IGTREE we have an arguably competitive efficient, but one-shot learning algorithm; IGTREE does not need an iterative procedure to set weights, and can also handle a large feature space. Instead of viewing all positional features as containers of thousands of atomic word features, it treats the positional features as the basic tests, branching on the word values in the tree.

More generally, as a precursor to the above-mentioned work, confusable disambiguation has been investigated in a string of papers discussing the application of various machine learning algorithms to the task (Yarowsky, 1994; Golding, 1995; Mangu and Brill, 1997; Huang and Powers, 2001).

6 Discussion

In this article we explored the scaling abilities of IGTREE, a simple decision-tree algorithm with favorable asymptotic complexities with respect to multi-label classification tasks. IGTREE is applied to word prediction, a task for which virtually unlimited amounts of training examples are available, with very large amounts of predictable class labels; and confusable disambiguation, a specialization of word prediction focusing on small sets of confusable words. Best results are 42.2% correctly predicted tokens (words and punctuation markers) when training and testing on data from the *Reuters* newswire corpus; and confusable disambiguation accuracies of well above 90%. Memory requirements and speeds were shown to be realistic.

Analysing the results of the learning curve experiments with increasing amounts of training examples, we observe that better word prediction accuracy can be attained simply by adding more training examples, and that the progress in accuracy proceeds at a log-linear rate. The best rate we observed was an 8% increase in performance every tenfold multiplication of the number of training examples, when training and testing on the same data.

Despite the fact that all-words prediction lags behind in disambiguating confusibles, in comparison with classifiers that are focused on disambiguating single sets of confusibles, we see that this lag is only relative to the amount of training material available.

Acknowledgements

This research was funded by the Netherlands Organisation for Scientific Research (NWO). The author wishes to thank Ko van der Sloot for programming assistance.

References

M. Banko and E. Brill. 2001. Scaling to very very large corpora for natural language disambiguation. In *Proceedings of the 39th Annual Meeting of the Association for Computational Linguistics*, pages 26–33. Association for Computational Linguistics.

L. Carroll. 1865. *Alice's Adventures in Wonderland*. Project Gutenberg.

W. Daelemans, A. Van den Bosch, and A. Weijters. 1997. IGTree: using trees for compression and classification in lazy learning algorithms. *Artificial Intelligence Review*, 11:407–423.

W. Daelemans, A. Van den Bosch, and J. Zavrel. 1999. Forgetting exceptions is harmful in language learning. *Machine Learning, Special issue on Natural Language Learning*, 34:11–41.

Y. Even-Zohar and D. Roth. 2000. A classification approach to word prediction. In *Proceedings of the First North-American Conference on Computational Linguistics*, pages 124–131, New Brunswick, NJ. ACL.

A.R. Golding and D. Roth. 1999. A Winnow-Based Approach to Context-Sensitive Spelling Correction. *Machine Learning*, 34(1–3):107–130.

A. R. Golding. 1995. A Bayesian hybrid method for context-sensitive spelling correction. In *Proceedings of the 3rd workshop on very large corpora, ACL-95*.

J. H. Huang and D. W. Powers. 2001. Large scale experiments on correction of confused words. In *Australasian Computer Science Conference Proceedings*, pages 77–82, Queensland AU. Bond University.

F. Jelinek. 1998. *Statistical Methods for Speech Recognition*. The MIT Press, Cambridge, MA.

D. E. Knuth. 1973. *The art of computer programming*, volume 3: Sorting and searching. Addison-Wesley, Reading, MA.

H. Kučera and W. N. Francis. 1967. *Computational Analysis of Present-Day American English*. Brown University Press, Providence, RI.

L. Mangu and E. Brill. 1997. Automatic rule acquisition for spelling correction. In *Proceedings of the International Conference on Machine Learning*, pages 187–194.

M. Marcus, S. Santorini, and M. Marcinkiewicz. 1993. Building a Large Annotated Corpus of English: the Penn Treebank. *Computational Linguistics*, 19(2):313–330.

J.R. Quinlan. 1993. *C4.5: Programs for Machine Learning*. Morgan Kaufmann, San Mateo, CA.

D. Wu, Z. Sui, and J. Zhao. 1999. An information-based method for selecting feature types for word prediction. In *Proceedings of the Sixth European Conference on Speech Communication and Technology, EUROSPEECH'99*, Budapest.

D. Yarowsky. 1994. Decision lists for lexical ambiguity resolution: application to accent restoration in Spanish and French. In *Proceedings of the Annual Meeting of the ACL*, pages 88–95.

J. Zavrel and W. Daelemans. 1997. Memory-based learning: Using similarity for smoothing. In *Proceedings of the 35th Annual Meeting of the Association for Computational Linguistics*, pages 436–443.

A Probabilistic Search for the Best Solution Among Partially Completed Candidates

Filip Ginter, Aleksandr Mylläri, and Tapio Salakoski
Turku Centre for Computer Science (TUCS) and
Department of Information Technology
University of Turku
Lemminkäisenkatu 14 A
20520 Turku, Finland
`first.last@it.utu.fi`

Abstract

We consider the problem of identifying among many candidates a single best solution which jointly maximizes several domain-specific target functions. Assuming that the candidate solutions can be generated incrementally, we model the error in prediction due to the incompleteness of partial solutions as a normally distributed random variable. Using this model, we derive a probabilistic search algorithm that aims at finding the best solution without the necessity to complete and rank all candidate solutions. We do not assume a Viterbi-type decoding, allowing a wider range of target functions.

We evaluate the proposed algorithm on the problem of best parse identification, combining simple heuristic with more complex machine-learning based target functions. We show that the search algorithm is capable of identifying candidates with a very high score without completing a significant proportion of the candidate solutions.

1 Background

Most of the current NLP systems assume a pipeline architecture, where each level of analysis is implemented as a module that produces a single, locally optimal solution that is passed to the next module in the pipeline. There has recently been an increased interest in the application of joint inference, which identifies a solution that is globally optimal throughout the system and avoids some of the problems of the pipeline architecture, such as error propagation.

We assume, at least conceptually, a division of the joint inference problem into two subproblems: that of finding a set of solutions that are structurally compatible with each of the modules, and that of selecting the globally best of these structurally correct solutions. Many of the modules define a target function that scores the solutions by some domain criteria based on local knowledge. The globally best solution maximizes some combination of the target functions, for example a sum.

For illustration, consider a system comprising of two modules: a POS tagger and a parser. The POS tagger generates a set of tag sequences that are compatible with the sentence text. Further, it may implement a target function, based, for instance, on tag n-grams, that scores these sequences according to POS-centric criteria. The parser produces a set of candidate parses and typically also implements a target function that scores the parses based on their structural and lexical features. Each parse that is compatible with both the POS tagger and the parser is structurally correct. The best solution may be defined, for instance, as such a solution that maximizes the sum of the scores of the POS- and parser-centric target functions.

In practice, the set of structurally correct solutions may be computed, for example, through the intersection or composition of finite-state automata as in the formalism of finite-state intersection grammars (Koskenniemi, 1990). Finding the best so-

Workshop on Computationally Hard Problemsand Joint Inference in Speech and Language Processing, pages 33–40,
New York City, New York, June 2006.

lution may be implemented as a best-path search through Viterbi decoding, given a target function that satisfies the Viterbi condition.

Most of the recent approaches to NLP tasks like parse re-ranking make, however, use of feature-based representations and machine-learning induced target functions, which do not allow efficient search strategies that are guaranteed to find the global optimum. In general case, all structurally correct solutions have to be generated and scored by the target functions in order to guarantee that the globally optimal solution is found. Further, each of the various problems in natural language processing is typically approached with a different class of models, ranging from n-gram statistics to complex regressors and classifiers such as the support vector machines. These different approaches need to be combined in order to find the globally optimal solution. Therefore, in our study we aim to develop a search strategy that allows to combine a wider range of target functions.

An alternative approach is that of propagating n best solutions through the pipeline system, where each step re-ranks the solutions by local criteria (Ji et al., 2005). Incorporating a wide range of features representing information from all levels of analysis into a single master classifier is other commonly used method (Kambhatla, 2004; Zelenko et al., 2004).

In this paper, we assume the possibility of generating the structurally correct solutions incrementally, through a sequence of partially completed solutions. We then derive a probabilistic search algorithm that attempts to identify the globally best solution, without fully completing all structurally correct solutions. Further, we do not impose strong restrictions, such as the Viterbi assumption, on the target functions.

To a certain extent, this approach is related to the problem of cost-sensitive learning, where obtaining a feature value is associated with a cost and the objective is to minimize the cost of training data acquisition and the cost of instance classification (Melville et al., 2004). However, the crucial difference is that we do not assume the possibility to influence when advancing a partial solution, which feature will be obtained next.

2 Method

Let us consider a system in which there are N solutions $s_1, \ldots, s_N \in \mathcal{S}$ to a problem and M target functions $f_1, \ldots, f_M$, where $f_k : \mathcal{S} \rightarrow \mathbb{R}$, that assign a score to each of the solutions. The score $f_k(s_i)$ expresses the extent to which the solution s_i satisfies the criterion implemented by the target function f_k. The overall score of a solution s_i

$$f(s_i) = \sum_{k=1}^{M} f_k(s_i) \tag{1}$$

is the sum of the scores given by the individual target functions. The objective is to identify $\hat{s}$, the best among the N possible solutions, that maximizes the overall score:

$$\hat{s} = \arg\max_{s_i} f(s_i) \ . \tag{2}$$

Suppose that the solutions are generated incrementally so that each solution s_i can be reached through a sequence of F *partial solutions* $s_{i,1}, s_{i,2}, \ldots, s_{i,F}$, where $s_{i,F} = s_i$. Let further $u : \mathcal{S} \rightarrow (0, 1]$ be a measure of a *degree of completion* for a particular solution. For a complete solution s_i, $u(s_i) = 1$, and for a partial solution $s_{i,n}$, $u(s_i) < 1$. For instance, when assigning POS tags to the words of a sentence, the degree of completion could be defined as the number of words assigned with a POS tag so far, divided by the total number of words in the sentence.

The score of a partial solution $s_{i,n}$ is, to a certain extent, a prediction of the score of the corresponding complete solution s_i. Intuitively, the accuracy of this prediction depends on the degree of completion. The score of a partial solution with a high degree of completion is generally closer to the final score, compared to a partial solution with a low degree of completion.

Let

$$\delta_k(s_{i,n}) = f_k(s_i) - f_k(s_{i,n}) \tag{3}$$

be the difference between the scores of s_i and $s_{i,n}$. That is, $\delta_k(s_{i,n})$ is the error in score caused by the incompleteness of the partial solution $s_{i,n}$. As the solutions are generated incrementally, the exact value of $\delta_k(s_{i,n})$ is not known at the moment of generating $s_{i,n}$ because the solution s_i has not been completed yet. However, we can model the error based on the knowledge of $s_{i,n}$. We assume that, for a given $s_{i,n}$, the error $\delta_k(s_{i,n})$ is a random variable distributed according to a probability distribution with a density function Δ_k, denoted as

$$\delta_k(s_{i,n}) \sim \Delta_k(\delta; s_{i,n}) \; . \tag{4}$$

The partial solution $s_{i,n}$ is a parameter to the distribution and, in theory, each partial solution gives rise to a different distribution of the same general shape.

We assume that the error $\delta(s_{i,n})$ is distributed around a mean value and for a 'reasonably behaving' target function, the probability of a small error is higher than the probability of a large error. Ideally, the target function will not exhibit any systematic error, and the mean value would thus be zero[1]. For instance, a positive mean error indicates a systematic bias toward underestimating the score. The mean error should approach 0 as the degree of completion increases and the error of a complete solution is always 0. We have further argued that the reliability of the prediction grows with the degree of completion. That is, the error of a partial solution with a high degree of completion should exhibit a smaller variance, compared to that of a largely incomplete solution. The variance of the error for a complete solution is always 0.

Knowing the distribution Δ_k of the error δ_k, the density of the distribution $d_k(f; s_{i,n})$ of the final score $f_k(s_i)$ is obtained by shifting the density of the error $\delta_k(s_{i,n})$ by $f_k(s_{i,n})$, that is,

$$f_k(s_i) \sim d_k(f; s_{i,n}) \; , \tag{5}$$

where

$$d_k(f; s_{i,n}) = \Delta_k(f - f_k(s_{i,n}); s_{i,n}) \; . \tag{6}$$

So far, we have discussed the case of a single target function f_k. Let us now consider the general case of M target functions. Knowing the final score density d_k for the individual target functions f_k, it is now necessary to find the density of the overall score $f(s_i)$. By Equation 1, it is distributed as the sum of the random variables $f_1(s_i), \ldots, f_M(s_i)$. Therefore, assuming independence, its density is the convolution of the densities of these variables, that is, given $s_{i,n}$,

$$d(f; s_{i,n}) = (d_1 * \ldots * d_M)(f; s_{i,n}) \; , \tag{7}$$

and

$$f(s_i) \sim d(f; s_{i,n}) \; . \tag{8}$$

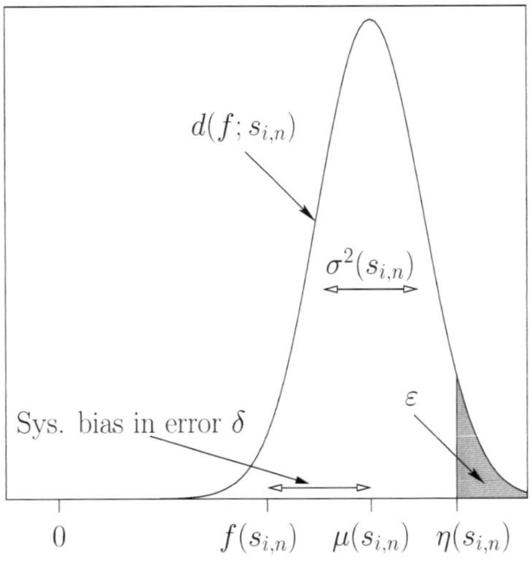

Figure 1: The probability density $d(f; s_{i,n})$ of the distribution of the final score $f(s_i)$, given a partial solution $s_{i,n}$. The density is assumed normally distributed, with mean $\mu(s_{i,n})$ and variance $\sigma^2(s_{i,n})$. With probability $1 - \varepsilon$, the final score is less than $\eta(s_{i,n})$.

We have assumed the independence of the target function scores. Further, we will make the assumption that d takes the form of the normal distribution, which is convolution-closed, a property necessary for efficient calculation by Equation 7. We thus have

$$d(f; s_{i,n}) = n\big(f; \mu(s_{i,n}), \sigma^2(s_{i,n})\big) \; , \tag{9}$$

where n is the normal density function. While it is unlikely that independence and normality hold strictly, it is a commonly used approximation, necessary for an analytical solution of (7). The notions introduced so far are illustrated in Figure 1.

2.1 The search algorithm

We will now apply the model introduced in the previous section to derive a probabilistic search algorithm.

[1] We will see in our evaluation experiments that this is not the case, and the target functions may exhibit a systematic bias in the error δ.

Let us consider two partial solutions $s_{i,n}$ and $s_{j,m}$ with the objective of deciding which one of them is 'more promising', that is, more likely to lead to a complete solution with a higher score. The condition of 'more promising' can be defined in several ways. For instance, once again assuming independence, it is possible to directly compute the probability $P(f(s_i) < f(s_j))$:

$$\begin{aligned} & P(f(s_i) < f(s_j)) \\ & = P(f(s_i) - f(s_j) < 0) \\ & = \int_{-\infty}^{0} (d_{s_{i,n}} * (-d_{s_{j,m}}))(f)\, df \,, \end{aligned} \tag{10}$$

where $d_{s_{i,n}}$ refers to the function $d(f; s_{i,n})$. Since d is the convolution-closed normal density, Equation 10 can be directly computed using the normal cumulative distribution. The disadvantage of this definition is that the cumulative distribution needs to be evaluated separately for each pair of partial solutions. Therefore, we assume an alternate definition of 'more promising' in which the cumulative distribution is evaluated only once for each partial solution.

Let $\varepsilon \in [0, 1]$ be a probability value and $\eta(s_{i,n})$ be the score such that $P(f(s_i) > \eta(s_{i,n})) = \varepsilon$. The value of $\eta(s_{i,n})$ can easily be computed from the inverse cumulative distribution function corresponding to the density function $d(f; s_{i,n})$. The interpretation of $\eta(s_{i,n})$ is that with probability of $1 - \varepsilon$, the partial solution $s_{i,n}$, once completed, will lead to a score smaller than $\eta(s_{i,n})$. The constant ε is a parameter, set to an appropriate small value. See Figure 1 for illustration.

We will refer to $\eta(s_{i,n})$ as the *maximal expected score* of $s_{i,n}$. Of the two partial solutions, we consider as 'more promising' the one, whose maximal expected score is higher. As illustrated in Figure 2, it is possible for a partial solution $s_{i,n}$ to be more promising even though its score $f(s_{i,n})$ is lower than that of some other partial solution $s_{j,m}$.

Further, given a complete solution s_i and a partial solution $s_{j,m}$, a related question is whether $s_{j,m}$ is a *promising solution*, that is, whether it is likely that advancing it will lead to a score higher than $f(s_i)$. Using the notion of maximal expected score, we say that a solution is promising if $\eta(s_{j,m}) > f(s_i)$.

With the definitions introduced so far, we are now able to perform two basic operations: compare two partial solutions, deciding which one of them is more promising, and compare a partial solution with some complete solution, deciding whether the partial solution is still promising or can be disregarded. These two basic operations are sufficient to devise the following search algorithm.

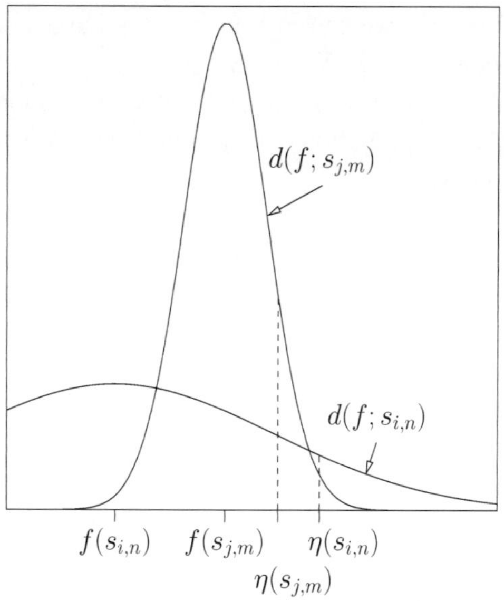

Figure 2: Although the score of $s_{i,n}$ is lower than the score of $s_{j,m}$, the partial solution $s_{i,n}$ is more promising, since $\eta(s_{i,n}) > \eta(s_{j,m})$. Note that for the sake of simplicity, a zero systematic bias of the error δ is assumed, that is, the densities are centered around the partial solution scores.

- Maintain a priority queue of partial solutions, ordered by their maximal expected score.
- In each step, remove from the queue the partial solution with the highest maximal expected score, advance it, and enqueue any resulting partial solutions.
- Iterate while the maximal expected score of the most promising partial solution remains higher than the score of the best complete solution discovered so far.

The parameter ε primarily affects how early the algorithm stops, however, it influences the order in which the solutions are considered as well. Low values of ε result in higher maximal expected scores and therefore partial solutions need to be advanced to a higher degree of completion before they can be disregarded as unpromising.

While there are no particular theoretical restrictions on the target functions, there is an important practical consideration. Since the target function is evaluated every time a partial solution $s_{i,n}$ is advanced into $s_{i,n+1}$, being able to use the information about $s_{i,n}$ to efficiently compute $f_k(s_{i,n+1})$ is necessary.

The algorithm is to a large extent related to the A* search algorithm, which maintains a priority queue of partial solutions, ordered according to a score $g(x) + h(x)$, where $g(x)$ is the score of x and $h(x)$ is a heuristic overestimate[2] of the final score of the goal reached from x. Here, the maximal expected score of a partial solution is an overestimate with the probability of $1 - \varepsilon$ and can be viewed as a probabilistic counterpart of the A* heuristic component $h(x)$. Note that A* only guarantees to find the best solution if $h(x)$ never underestimates, which is not the case here.

2.2 Estimation of $\mu_k(s_{i,n})$ and $\sigma_k^2(s_{i,n})$

So far, we have assumed that for each partial solution $s_{i,n}$ and each target function f_k, the density $\Delta_k(\delta; s_{i,n})$ is defined as a normal density specified by the mean $\mu_k(s_{i,n})$ and variance $\sigma_k^2(s_{i,n})$. This density models the error $\delta_k(s_{i,n})$ that arises due to the incompleteness of $s_{i,n}$. The parameters $\mu_k(s_{i,n})$ and $\sigma_k^2(s_{i,n})$ are, in theory, different for each $s_{i,n}$ and reflect the behavior of the target function f_k as well as the degree of completion and possibly other attributes of $s_{i,n}$. It is thus necessary to estimate these two parameters from data.

Let us, for each target function f_k, consider a training set of observations $\mathcal{T}_k \subset \mathcal{S} \times \mathbb{R}$. Each training observation $t_j = \left(s_{j,n_j}, \delta_k\left(s_{j,n_j}\right)\right) \in \mathcal{T}_k$ corresponds to a solution s_{j,n_j} with a known error $\delta_k\left(s_{j,n_j}\right) = f_k(s_j) - f_k\left(s_{j,n_j}\right)$.

Before we introduce the method to estimate the density $\Delta_k(\delta; s_{i,n})$ for a particular $s_{i,n}$, we discuss data normalization. The overall score $f(s_{i,n})$ is defined as the sum of the scores assigned by the individual target functions f_k. Naturally, it is desirable that these scores are of comparable magnitudes. Therefore, we normalize the target functions using the z-normalization

$$z(x) = \frac{x - mean(x)}{stdev(x)} \ . \tag{11}$$

Each target function f_k is normalized separately, based on the data in the training set $\mathcal{T}_k$. Throughout our experiments, the values of the target function are always z-normalized.

Let us now consider the estimation of the mean $\mu_k(s_{i,n})$ and variance $\sigma_k^2(s_{i,n})$ that define the density $\Delta_k(\delta; s_{i,n})$. Naturally, it is not possible to estimate the distribution parameters for each solution $s_{i,n}$ separately. Instead, we approximate the parameters based on two most salient characteristics of each solution: the degree of completion $u(s_{i,n})$ and the score $f_k(s_{i,n})$. Thus,

$$\mu_k(s_{i,n}) \approx \mu_k(u(s_{i,n}), f_k(s_{i,n})) \tag{12}$$

$$\sigma_k^2(s_{i,n}) \approx \sigma_k^2(u(s_{i,n}), f_k(s_{i,n})) \ . \tag{13}$$

Let us assume the following notation: $u_i = u(s_{i,n})$, $f_i = f_k(s_{i,n})$, $u_j = u\left(s_{j,n_j}\right)$, $f_j = f_k\left(s_{j,n_j}\right)$, and $\delta_j = \delta_k\left(s_{j,n_j}\right)$. The estimate is obtained from $\mathcal{T}_k$ using kernel smoothing (Silverman, 1986):

$$\mu_k(u_i, f_i) = \frac{\sum_{t_j \in \mathcal{T}} \delta_j K}{\sum_{t_j \in \mathcal{T}} K} \tag{14}$$

and

$$\sigma_k^2(u_i, f_i) = \frac{\sum_{t_j \in \mathcal{T}} (\delta_j - \mu_k(u_i, f_i))^2 K}{\sum_{t_j \in \mathcal{T}} K} \ , \tag{15}$$

where K stands for the kernel value $K_{u_i, f_i}(u_j, f_j)$. The kernel K is the product of two Gaussians, centered at u_i and f_i, respectively.

$$K_{u_i, f_i}(u_j, f_j) = n\left(u_j; u_i, \sigma_u^2\right) \cdot n\left(f_j; f_i, \sigma_f^2\right) \ , \tag{16}$$

where $n\left(x; \mu, \sigma^2\right)$ is the normal density function. The variances σ_u^2 and σ_f^2 control the degree of smoothing along the u and f axes, respectively. High variance results in stronger smoothing, compared to low variance. In our evaluation, we set the

[2] In the usual application of A* to shortest-path search, $h(x)$ is a heuristic underestimate since the objective is to minimize the score.

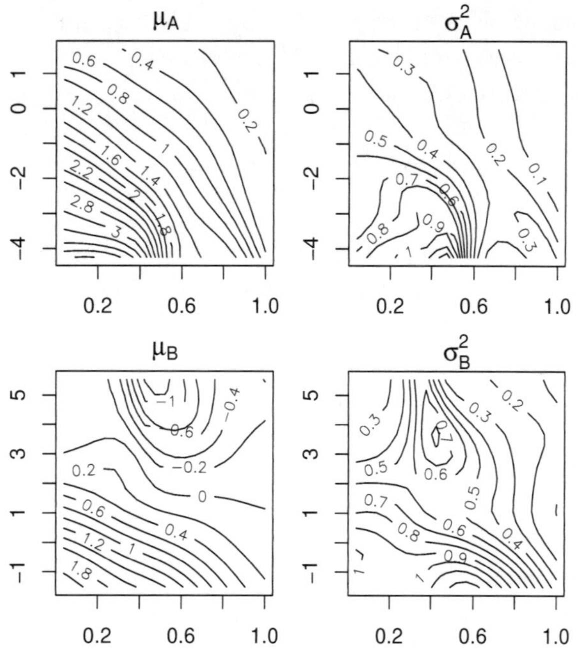

Figure 3: Mean and variance of the error $\delta(s_{i,n})$. By (12) and (13), the error is approximated as a function of the degree of completion $u(s_{i,n})$ and the score $f_k(s_{i,n})$. The degree of completion is on the horizontal and the score on the vertical axis. The estimates (μ_A, σ_A^2) and (μ_B, σ_B^2) correspond to the RLSC regressor and average link length target functions, respectively.

variance such that σ_u and σ_f equal to 10% of the distance from $\min(u_j)$ to $\max(u_j)$ and from $\min(f_j)$ to $\max(f_j)$, respectively.

The kernel-smoothed estimates of μ and σ^2 for two of the four target functions used in the evaluation experiments are illustrated in Figure 3. While both estimates demonstrate the decrease both in mean and variance for u approaching 0, the target functions generally exhibit a different behavior. Note that the values are clearly dependent on both the score and the degree of completion, indicating that the degree of completion alone is not sufficiently representative of the partial solutions. Ideally, the values of both the mean and variance should be strictly 0 for $u = 1$, however, due to the effect of smoothing, they remain non-zero.

3 Evaluation

We test the proposed search algorithm on the problem of dependency parsing. We have previously developed a finite-state implementation (Ginter et al., 2006) of the Link Grammar (LG) parser (Sleator and Temperley, 1991) which generates the parse through the intersection of several finite-state automata. The resulting automaton encodes all candidate parses. The parses are then generated from left to right, proceeding through the automaton from the initial to the final state. A partial parse is a sequence of n words from the beginning of the sentence, together with string encoding of their dependencies. Advancing a partial parse corresponds to appending to it the next word. The degree of completion is then defined as the number of words currently generated in the parse, divided by the total number of words in the sentence.

To evaluate the ability of the proposed method to combine diverse criteria in the search, we use four target functions: a complex state-of-the-art parse reranker based on a regularized least-squares (RLSC) regressor (Tsivtsivadze et al., 2005), and three measures inspired by the simple heuristics applied by the LG parser. The criteria are the average length of a dependency, the average level of nesting of a dependency, and the average number of dependencies linking a word. The RLSC regressor, on the other hand, employs complex features and word n-gram statistics.

The dataset consists of 200 sentences randomly selected from the BioInfer corpus of dependency-parsed sentences extracted from abstracts of biomedical research articles (Pyysalo et al., 2006). For each sentence, we have randomly selected a maximum of 100 parses. For sentences with less than 100 parses, all parses were selected. The average number of parses per sentence is 62. Further, we perform 5×2 cross-validation, that is, in each of five replications, we divide the data randomly to two sets of 100 sentences and use one set to estimate the probability distributions and the other set to measure the performance of the search algorithm. The RLSC regressor is trained once, using a different set of sentences from the BioInfer corpus. The results presented here are averaged over the 10 folds. As a comparative baseline, we use a simple greedy search algorithm that always advances the partial solution with the highest score until all solutions have been generated.

3.1 Results

For each sentence s with parses $\mathcal{S}\{s_1, \ldots, s_N\}$, let $\mathcal{S}_C \subseteq \mathcal{S}$ be the subset of parses fully completed before the algorithm stops and $\mathcal{S}_N = \mathcal{S} \setminus \mathcal{S}_C$ the subset of parses not fully completed. Let further T_C be the number of iterations taken before the algorithm stops, and T be the total number of steps needed to generate all parses in $\mathcal{S}$. Thus, $|\mathcal{S}|$ is the size of the search space measured in the number of parses, and T is the size of the search space measured in the number of steps. For a single parse s_i, $rank(s_i)$ is the number of parses in $\mathcal{S}$ with a score higher than $f(s_i)$ plus 1. Thus, the rank of all solutions with the maximal score is 1. Finally, $ord(s_i)$ corresponds to the order in which the parses were completed by the algorithm (disregarding the stopping criterion). For example, if the parses were completed in the order s_3, s_8, s_1, then $ord(s_3) = 1$, $ord(s_8) = 2$, and $ord(s_1) = 3$. While two solutions have the same rank if their scores are equal, no two solutions have the same order. The best completed solution $\hat{s}_C \in \mathcal{S}_C$ is the solution with the highest rank in $\mathcal{S}_C$ and the lowest order among solutions with the same rank. The best solution $\hat{s}$ is the solution with rank 1 and the lowest order among solutions with rank 1. If $\hat{s} \in \mathcal{S}_C$, then $\hat{s}_C = \hat{s}$ and the objective of the algorithm to find the best solution was fulfilled. We use the following measures of performance: $rank(\hat{s}_C)$, $ord(\hat{s})$, $\frac{|\mathcal{S}_C|}{|\mathcal{S}|}$, and $\frac{T_C}{T}$. The most important criteria are $rank(\hat{s}_C)$ which measures how good the best found solution is, and $\frac{T_C}{T}$ which measures the proportion of steps actually taken by the algorithm of the total number of steps needed to complete all the candidate solutions. Further, $ord(\hat{s})$, the number of parses completed before the global optimum was reached regardless the stopping criterion, is indicative about the ability of the search to reach the global optimum early among the completed parses. Note that all measures except for $ord(\hat{s})$ equal to 1 for the baseline greedy search, since it lacks a stopping criterion.

The average performance values for four settings of the parameter ε are presented in Table 1. Clearly,

ε	$rank(\hat{s}_C)$	$ord(\hat{s})$	$\frac{\lvert\mathcal{S}_C\rvert}{\lvert\mathcal{S}\rvert}$	$\frac{T_C}{T}$
0.01	1.6	8.8	0.78	0.94
0.05	2.8	11.2	0.62	0.85
0.10	4.0	12.2	0.53	0.79
0.20	6.0	13.5	0.41	0.73
Base	1.0	28.7	1.00	1.00

Table 1: Average results over all sentences.

the algorithm behaves as expected with respect to the parameter ε. While with the strictest setting $\varepsilon = 0.01$, 94% of the search space is explored, with the least strict setting of $\varepsilon = 0.2$, 73% is explored, thus pruning one quarter of the search space. The proportion of completed parses is generally considerably lower than the proportion of explored search space. This indicates that the parses are generally advanced to a significant level of completion, but then ruled out. The behavior of the algorithm is thus closer to a breadth-first, rather than depth-first search. We also notice that the average rank of the best completed solution is very low, indicating that although the algorithm does not necessarily identify the best solution, it generally identifies a very good solution. In addition, the order of the best solution is low as well, suggesting that generally good solutions are identified before low-score solutions. Further, compared to the baseline, the globally optimal solution is reached earlier among the completed parses, although this does not imply that it is reached earlier in the number of steps. Apart from the overall averages, we also consider the performance with respect to the number of alternative parses for each sentence (Table 2). Here we see that even with the least strict setting, the search finds a reasonably good solution while being able to reduce the search space to 48%.

4 Conclusions and future work

We have considered the problem of identifying a globally optimal solution among a set of candidate solutions, jointly optimizing several target functions that implement domain criteria. Assuming the solutions are generated incrementally, we have derived a probabilistic search algorithm that aims to identify the globally optimal solution without completing all of the candidate solutions. The algorithm is based on a model of the error in prediction caused by the in-

$\|S\|$	#	$\varepsilon = 0.01$ $rank(\hat{s}_C)$	$ord(\hat{s})$	$\frac{\|S_C\|}{\|S\|}$	$\frac{T_C}{T}$	$\varepsilon = 0.2$ $rank(\hat{s}_C)$	$ord(\hat{s})$	$\frac{\|S_C\|}{\|S\|}$	$\frac{T_C}{T}$	Base $ord(\hat{s})$
1-10	40	1.0	1.6	1.00	1.00	1.2	1.8	0.84	0.95	2.85
11-20	18	1.1	4.4	0.88	0.97	2.8	7.0	0.54	0.79	9.82
21-30	8	1.0	2.9	1.00	1.00	1.0	2.4	0.80	0.98	14.75
31-40	9	1.2	7.8	0.79	0.95	2.6	10.8	0.48	0.74	20.67
41-50	6	1.0	4.4	0.80	0.89	4.9	9.8	0.28	0.61	18.07
51-60	3	1.0	2.3	0.64	0.88	7.1	5.9	0.30	0.59	38.67
61-70	5	1.1	26.9	0.86	0.99	3.4	23.2	0.22	0.68	32.60
71-80	3	1.0	8.7	0.78	0.98	9.2	19.6	0.30	0.71	49.67
81-90	6	2.5	8.2	0.61	0.94	9.3	16.6	0.24	0.76	47.67
91-100	102	5.2	20.9	0.50	0.81	18.9	38.2	0.15	0.48	52.69

Table 2: Average results with respect to the number of alternative parses. The column # contains the number of sentences in the dataset which have the given number of parses.

completeness of a partial solution. Using the model, the order in which partial solutions are explored is defined, as well as a stopping criterion for the algorithm.

We have performed an evaluation using best parse identification as the model problem. The results indicate that the method is capable of combining simple heuristic criteria with a complex regressor, identifying solutions with a very low average rank.

The crucial component of the method is the model of the error δ. Improving the accuracy of the model may potentially further improve the performance of the algorithm, allowing a more accurate stopping criterion and better order in which the parses are completed. We have assumed independence between the scores assigned by the target functions. As a future work, a multivariate model will be considered that takes into account the mutual dependencies of the target functions.

References

Filip Ginter, Sampo Pyysalo, Jorma Boberg, and Tapio Salakoski. 2006. Regular approximation of Link Grammar. Manuscript under review.

Heng Ji, David Westbrook, and Ralph Grishman. 2005. Using semantic relations to refi ne coreference decisions. In *Proceedings of Human Language Technology Conference and Conference on Empirical Methods in Natural Language Processing (HLT/EMNLP'05), Vancouver, Canada*, pages 17–24. ACL.

Nanda Kambhatla. 2004. Combining lexical, syntactic, and semantic features with maximum entropy models for information extraction. In *The Companion Volume to the Proceedings of 42st Annual Meeting of the Association for Computational Linguistics (ACL'04), Barcelona, Spain*, pages 178–181. ACL.

Kimmo Koskenniemi. 1990. Finite-state parsing and disambiguation. In *Proceedings of the 13th International Conference on Computational Linguistics (COLING'90), Helsinki, Finland*, pages 229–232. ACL.

Prem Melville, Maytal Saar-Tsechansky, Foster Provost, and Raymond Mooney. 2004. Active feature-value acquisition for classifi er induction. In *Proceedings of the Fourth IEEE International Conference on Data Mining (ICDM'04)*, pages 483–486. IEEE Computer Society.

Sampo Pyysalo, Filip Ginter, Juho Heimonen, Jari Björne, Jorma Boberg, Jouni Järvinen, and Tapio Salakoski. 2006. Bio Information Extraction Resource: A corpus for information extraction in the biomedical domain. Manuscript under review.

Bernard W. Silverman. 1986. *Density Estimation for Statistics and Data Analysis*. Chapman & Hall.

Daniel D. Sleator and Davy Temperley. 1991. Parsing English with a link grammar. Technical Report CMU-CS-91-196, Department of Computer Science, Carnegie Mellon University, Pittsburgh, PA.

Evgeni Tsivtsivadze, Tapio Pahikkala, Sampo Pyysalo, Jorma Boberg, Aleksandr Mylläri, and Tapio Salakoski. 2005. Regularized least-squares for parse ranking. In *Proceedings of the 6th International Symposium on Intelligent Data Analysis (IDA'05), Madrid, Spain*, pages 464–474. Springer, Heidelberg.

Dmitry Zelenko, Chinatsu Aone, and Jason Tibbets. 2004. Binary integer programming for information extraction. In *Proceedings of the ACE Evaluation Meeting*.

Practical Markov Logic Containing First-Order Quantifiers with Application to Identity Uncertainty

Aron Culotta and **Andrew McCallum**
Department of Computer Science
University of Massachusetts
Amherst, MA 01003
{culotta, mccallum}@cs.umass.edu

Abstract

Markov logic is a highly expressive language recently introduced to specify the connectivity of a Markov network using first-order logic. While Markov logic is capable of constructing arbitrary first-order formulae over the data, the complexity of these formulae is often limited in practice because of the size and connectivity of the resulting network. In this paper, we present approximate inference and estimation methods that incrementally instantiate portions of the network as needed to enable first-order existential and universal quantifiers in *Markov logic networks*. When applied to the problem of identity uncertainty, this approach results in a conditional probabilistic model that can reason about objects, combining the expressivity of recently introduced BLOG models with the predictive power of conditional training. We validate our algorithms on the tasks of citation matching and author disambiguation.

1 Introduction

Markov logic networks (MLNs) combine the probabilistic semantics of graphical models with the expressivity of first-order logic to model relational dependencies (Richardson and Domingos, 2004). They provide a method to instantiate Markov networks from a set of constants and first-order formulae.

While MLNs have the power to specify Markov networks with complex, finely-tuned dependencies, the difficulty of instantiating these networks grows with the complexity of the formulae. In particular, expressions with first-order quantifiers can lead to networks that are large and densely connected, making exact probabilistic inference intractable. Because of this, existing applications of MLNs have not exploited the full richness of expressions available in first-order logic.

For example, consider the database of researchers described in Richardson and Domingos (2004), where predicates include PROFESSOR(PERSON), STUDENT(PERSON), ADVISEDBY(PERSON, PERSON), and PUBLISHED(AUTHOR, PAPER). First-order formulae include statements such as "students are not professors" and "each student has at most one advisor." Consider instead statements such as "all the students of an advisor publish papers with similar words in the title" or "this subset of students belong to the same lab." To instantiate an MLN with such predicates requires existential and universal quantifiers, resulting in either a densely connected network, or a network with prohibitively many nodes. (In the latter example, it may be necessary to ground the predicate for each element of the power set of students.)

However, as discussed in Section 2, there may be cases where these *aggregate predicates* increase predictive power. For example, in predicting the value of HAVESAMEADVISOR($a_i \ldots a_{i+k}$), it may be useful to know the values of aggregate evidence predicates such as COAUTHOREDATLEASTTWOPAPERS($a_i \ldots a_{i+k}$), which indicates whether there are at least two papers that some combination of authors from $a_i \ldots a_{i+k}$ have co-authored. Additionally, we can construct predicates such as NUMBEROFSTUDENTS(a_i) to model the number of students a researcher is likely to advise simultaneously.

These aggregate predicates are examples of universal and existentially quantified predicates over observed and unobserved values. To enable these sorts

Workshop on Computationally Hard Problemsand Joint Inference in Speech and Language Processing, pages 41–48,
New York City, New York, June 2006.

of predicates while limiting the complexity of the ground Markov network, we present an algorithm that incrementally expands the set of aggregate predicates during the inference procedure. In this paper, we describe a general algorithm for incremental expansion of predicates in MLNs, then present an implementation of the algorithm applied to the problem of identity uncertainty.

2 Related Work

MLNs were designed to subsume various previously proposed statistical relational models. *Probabilistic relational models* (Friedman et al., 1999) combine descriptive logic with directed graphical models, but are restricted to acyclic graphs. *Relational Markov networks* (Taskar et al., 2002) use SQL queries to specify the structure of undirected graphical models. Since first-order logic subsumes SQL, MLNs can be viewed as more expressive than relational Markov networks, although existing applications of MLNs have not fully utilized this increased expressivity. Other approaches combining logic programming and log-linear models include *stochastic logic programs* (Cussens, 2003) and MACCENT(Dehaspe, 1997), although MLNs can be shown to represent both of these.

Viewed as a method to avoid grounding an intractable number of predicates, this paper has similar motivations to recent work in *lifted inference* (Poole, 2003; de Salvo Braz et al., 2005), which performs inference directly at the first-order level to avoid instantiating all predicates. Although our model is not an instance of lifted inference, it does attempt to reduce the number of predicates by instantiating them incrementally.

Identity uncertainty (also known as record linkage, deduplication, object identification, and co-reference resolution) is the problem of determining whether a set of constants (*mentions*) refer to the same object (*entity*). Successful identity resolution enables vision systems to track objects, database systems to deduplicate redundant records, and text processing systems to resolve disparate mentions of people, organizations, and locations.

Many probabilistic models of object identification have been proposed in the past 40 years in databases (Fellegi and Sunter, 1969; Winkler, 1993) and natural language processing (McCarthy and Lehnert, 1995; Soon et al., 2001). With the introduction of statistical relational learning, more sophisticated models of identity uncertainty have been developed that consider the dependencies between related consolidation decisions.

Most relevant to this work are the recent relational models of identity uncertainty (Milch et al., 2005; McCallum and Wellner, 2003; Parag and Domingos, 2004). McCallum and Wellner (2003) present experiments using a conditional random field that factorizes into a product of pairwise decisions about mention pairs (Model 3). These pairwise decisions are made collectively using relational inference; however, as pointed out in Milch et al. (2004), there are shortcomings to this model that stem from the fact that it does not capture features of *objects*, only of mention pairs. For example, aggregate features such as "a researcher is unlikely to publish in more than 2 different fields" or "a person is unlikely to be referred to by three different names" cannot be captured by solely examining pairs of mentions. Additionally, decomposing an object into a set of mention pairs results in "double-counting" of attributes, which can skew reasoning about a single object (Milch et al., 2004). Similar problems apply to the model in Parag and Domingos (2004).

Milch et al. (2005) address these issues by constructing a generative probabilistic model over possible worlds called BLOG, where realizations of objects are typically sampled from a generative process. While BLOG model provides attractive semantics for reasoning about unknown objects, the transition to generatively trained models sacrifices some of the attractive properties of the discriminative model in McCallum and Wellner (2003) and Parag and Domingos (2004), such as the ability to easily incorporate many overlapping features of the observed mentions. In contrast, generative models are constrained either to assume the independence of these features or to explicitly model their interactions.

Object identification can also be seen as an instance of *supervised clustering*. Daumé III and Marcu (2004) and Carbonetto et al. (2005) present similar Bayesian supervised clustering algorithms that use a Dirichlet process to model the number of clusters. As a generative model, it has similar advantages and disadvantages as Milch et al. (2005), with the added capability of integrating out the uncertainty in the true number of objects.

In this paper, we present of identity uncertainty that incorporates the attractive properties of McCallum and Wellner (2003) and Milch et al. (2005), resulting in a discriminative model to reason about objects.

3 Markov logic networks

Let $F = \{F_i\}$ be a set of first order formulae with corresponding real-valued weights $w = \{w_i\}$. Given a set of constants $C = \{c_i\}$, define $n_i(x)$ to be the number of true *groundings* of F_i realized in a setting of the world given by atomic formulae x. A Markov logic network (MLN) (Richardson and Domingos, 2004) defines a joint probability distribution over possible worlds x. In this paper, we will work with discriminative MLNs (Singla and Domingos, 2005), which define the conditional distribution over a set of query atoms y given a set of evidence atoms x. Using the normalizing constant Z_x, the conditional distribution is given by

$$P(Y = y|X = x) = \frac{1}{Z_x} \exp\left(\sum_{i=1}^{|F_y|} w_i n_i(x, y)\right) \quad (1)$$

where $F_y \subseteq F$ is the set of clauses for which at least one grounding contains a query atom, and $n_i(x, y)$ is the number of true groundings of the ith clause containing evidence atom x and query atom y.

3.1 Inference Complexity in Ground Markov Networks

The set of predicates and constants in Markov logic define the structure of a Markov network, called a *ground Markov network*. In discriminative Markov logic networks, this resulting network is a conditional Markov network (also known as a *conditional random field* (Lafferty et al., 2001)).

From Equation 1, the formulae F_y specify the structure of the corresponding Markov network as follows: Each grounding of a predicate specified in F_y has a corresponding node in the Markov network; and an edge connects two nodes in the network if and only if their corresponding predicates co-occur in a grounding of a formula F_y. Thus, the complexity of the formulae in F_y will determine the complexity of the resulting Markov network, and therefore the complexity of inference. When F_y contains complex first-order quantifiers, the resulting Markov network may contain a prohibitively large number of nodes.

For example, let the set of constants C be the set of authors $\{a_i\}$, papers $\{p_i\}$, and conferences $\{c_i\}$ from a research publication database. Predicates may include AUTHOROF(a_i, p_j), ADVISOROF(a_i, a_j), and PROGRAMCOMMITTEE(a_i, c_j). Each grounding of a predicate corresponds to a random variable in the corresponding Markov network.

It is important to notice how *query* predicates and *evidence* predicates differ in their impact on inference complexity. Grounded evidence predicates result in observed random variables that can be highly connected without resulting in an increase in inference complexity. For example, consider the binary evidence predicate HAVESAMELASTNAME$(a_i \ldots a_{i+k})$. This *aggregate* predicate reflects information about a subset of $(k - i + 1)$ constants. The value of this predicate is dependent on the values of HAVESAMELASTNAME(a_i, a_{i+1}), HAVESAMELASTNAME(a_i, a_{i+2}), etc. However, since all of the corresponding variables are observed, inference does not need to ensure their consistency or model their interaction.

In contrast, complex *query* predicates can make inference more difficult. Consider the query predicate HAVESAMEADVISOR$(a_i \ldots a_{i+k})$. Here, the related predicates HAVESAMEADVISOR(a_i, a_{i+1}), HAVESAMEADVISOR(a_i, a_{i+2}), etc., all correspond to *unobserved* binary random variables that the model must predict. To ensure their consistency, the resulting Markov network must contain dependency edges between each of these variables, resulting in a densely connected network. Since inference in general in Markov networks scales exponentially with the size of the largest clique, inference in the grounded network quickly becomes intractable.

One solution is to limit the expressivity of the predicates. In the previous example, we can decompose the predicate HAVESAMEADVISOR$(a_i \ldots a_{i+k})$ into its $(k - i + 1)^2$ corresponding *pairwise* predicates, such as HAVESAMEADVISOR(a_i, a_{i+1}). Answering an aggregate query about the advisors of a group of students can be handled by a conjunction of these pairwise predicates.

However, as discussed in Sections 1 and 2, we would like to reason about *objects*, not just pairs of *mentions*, because this enables richer evidence predicates. For example, the evidence predicates ATLEASTTWOCOAUTHOREDPAPERS$(a_i \ldots a_{i+k})$ and NUMBEROFSTUDENTS(a_i) can be highly predictive of the query predicate HAVESAMEADVISOR$(a_i \ldots a_{i+k})$.

Below, we describe a discriminative MLN for identity uncertainty that is able to reason at the object level.

3.2 Identity uncertainty

Typically, MLNs make a *unique names* assumption, requiring that different constants refer to distinct objects. In the publications database example, each author constant a_i is a string representation of one author mention found in the text of a citation. The unique names assumption assumes that each a_i refers to a distinct author in the real-world. This simplifies the network structure at the risk of weak or fallacious predictions (e.g., ADVISOROF(a_i, a_j) is erroneous if a_i and a_j actually refer to the same author). The *identity uncertainty* problem is the task of removing the unique names assumption by determining which constants refer to the same real-world objects.

Richardson and Domingos (2004) address this concern by creating the predicate $\text{EQUALS}(c_i, c_j)$ between each pair of constants. While this retains the coherence of the model, the restriction to pairwise predicates can be a drawback if there exist informative features over sets of constants. In particular, by only capturing features of pairs of constants, this solution cannot model the compatibility of object attributes, only of constant attributes (Section 2).

Instead, we desire a conditional model that allows predicates to be defined over a set of constants.

One approach is to introduce constants that represent objects, and connect them to their mentions by predicates such as $\text{ISMENTIONOF}(c_i, c_j)$. In addition to computational issues, this approach also somewhat problematically requires choosing the number of objects. (See Richardson and Domingos (2004) for a brief discussion.)

Instead, we propose instantiating *aggregate predicates* over sets of constants, such that a setting of these predicates implicitly determines the number of objects. This approach allows us to model attributes over entire objects, rather than only pairs of constants. In the following sections, we describe aggregate predicates in more detail, as well as the approximations necessary to implement them efficiently.

3.3 Aggregate predicates

Aggregate predicates are predicates that take as arguments an arbitrary number of constants. For example, the $\text{HAVESAMEADVISOR}(a_i \ldots a_{i+k})$ predicate in the previous section is an example of an aggregate predicate over $k - i + 1$ constants.

Let $I_C = \{1 \ldots N\}$ be the set of indices into the set of constants C, with power set $\mathcal{P}(I_C)$. For any subset $\mathbf{d} \in \mathcal{P}(I_C)$, an aggregate predicate $\text{A}(\mathbf{d})$ defines a property over the subset of constants $\mathbf{d}$.

Note that aggregate predicates can be translated into first-order formulae. For example, $\text{HAVESAMEADVISOR}(a_i \ldots a_{i+k})$ can be re-written as $\forall(a_x, a_y) \in \{a_i \ldots a_{i+k}\}\ \text{SAMEADVISOR}(a_x, a_y)$. By using aggregate predicates we make explicit the fact that we are modeling the attributes at the object level.

We distinguish between *aggregate query predicates*, which represent unobserved aggregate variables, and *aggregate evidence predicates*, which represent observed aggregate variables. Note that using aggregate *query* predicates can complicate inference, since they represent a collection of fully connected hidden variables. The main point of this paper is that although these aggregate query predicates are specifiable in MLNs, they have not been utilized because of the resulting inference complexity. We show that the gains made possible by these predicates often outweigh the approximations required for inference.

As discussed in Section 3.1, for each aggregate query predicates $\text{A}(\mathbf{d})$, it is critical that the model predict consistent values for every related subset of $\mathbf{d}$. Enforcing this consistency requires introducing dependency edges between aggregate query predicates that share arguments. In general, this can be a difficult problem. Here, we focus on the special case for identity uncertainty where the main query predicate under consideration is $\text{AREEQUAL}(\mathbf{d})$.

The aggregate query predicate $\text{AREEQUAL}(\mathbf{d})$ is true if and only if all constants $d_i \in \mathbf{d}$ refer to the same object. Since each subset of constants corresponds to a candidate object, a (consistent) setting of all the AREEQUAL predicates results in a solution to the object identification problem. The number of objects is chosen based on the optimal grounding of each of these aggregate predicates, and therefore does not require a prior over the number of objects. That is, once all the AREEQUAL predicates are set, they determine a clustering with a fixed number of objects. The number of objects is not modeled or set directly, but is implied by the result of MAP inference. (However, a posterior over the number of objects could be modeled discriminatively in an MLN (Richardson and Domingos, 2004).)

This formulation also allows us to compute aggregate evidence predicates over objects to help predict the values of each AREEQUAL predicate. For example, $\text{NUMBERFIRSTNAMES}(\mathbf{d})$ returns the number of different first names used to refer to the object referenced by constants $\mathbf{d}$. In this way, we can model aggregate features of an object, capturing the compatibility among its attributes.

For a given C, there are $|\mathcal{P}(I_C)|$ possible groundings of the AREEQUAL query predicates. Naively implemented, such an approach would require enumerating all subsets of constants, ultimately resulting in an unwieldy network.

An equivalent way to state the problem is that using N-ary predicates results in a Markov network with one node for each grounding of the predicate. Since in the general case there is one grounding for each subset of C, the size of the corresponding Markov network will be exponential in $|C|$. See Figure 1 for an example instantiation of an MLN with three constants (a, b, c) and one AREEQUAL predicate.

In this paper, we provide algorithms to perform approximate inference and parameter estimation by incrementally instantiating these predicates

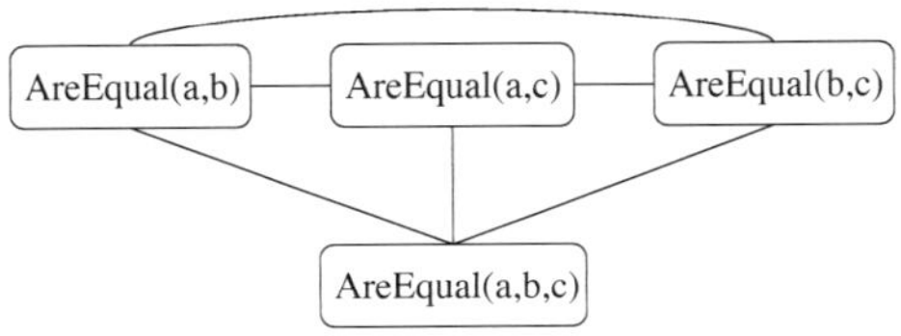

Figure 1: An example of the network instantiated by an MLN with three constants and the aggregate predicate AREEQUAL, instantiated for all possible subsets with size ≥ 2.

as needed.

3.4 MAP Inference

Maximum a posteriori (MAP) inference seeks the solution to

$$y^* = \underset{y}{\operatorname{argmax}}\, P(Y = y|X = x)$$

where y^* is the setting of all the query predicates F_y (e.g. AREEQUAL) with the maximal conditional density.

In large, densely connected Markov networks, a common approximate inference technique is loopy belief propagation (i.e. the *max-product* algorithm applied to a cyclic graph). However, the use of aggregate predicates makes it intractable even to instantiate the entire network, making max-product an inappropriate solution.

Instead, we employ an incremental inference technique that grounds aggregate query predicates in an agglomerative fashion based on the model's current MAP estimates. This algorithm can be viewed as a greedy agglomerative search for a local optimum of $P(Y|X)$, and has connections to recent work on *correlational clustering* (Bansal et al., 2004) and graph partitioning for MAP estimation (Boykov et al., 2001).

First, note that finding the MAP estimate does not require computing Z_x, since we are only interested in the *relative* values of each configuration, and Z_x is fixed for a given x. Thus, at iteration t, we compute an unnormalized score for y^t (the current setting of the query predicates) given the evidence predicates x as follows:

$$S(y^t, x) = \exp\left(\sum_{i=0}^{|F^t|} w_i n_i(x, y^t)\right)$$

where $F^t \subseteq F_y$ is the set of aggregate predicates representing a partial solution to the object identification task for constants C, specified by y^t.

Algorithm 1 Approximate MAP Inference Algorithm

1: Given initial predicates F^0
2: **while** ScoreIsIncreased **do**
3: $\quad F_i^* \Leftarrow$ FindMostLikelyPredicate(F^t)
4: $\quad F_i^* \Leftarrow$ **true**
5: $\quad F^t \Leftarrow$ ExpandPredicates(F_i^*, F^t)
6: **end while**

Algorithm 1 outlines a high-level description of the approximate MAP inference algorithm. The algorithm first initializes the set of query predicated F^0 such that all AREEQUAL predicates are restricted to pairs of constants, i.e. AREEQUAL(c_i, c_j) $\forall(i, j)$. This is equivalent to a Markov network containing one unobserved random variable for each pair of constants, where each variable indicates whether a pair of constants refer to the same object.

Initially, each AREEQUAL predicate is assumed false. In line 3, the procedure FINDMOSTLIKELYPREDICATE iterates through each query predicate in F^t, setting each to true in turn and calculating its impact on the scoring function. The procedure returns the predicate F_i^* such that setting F_i^* to TRUE results in the greatest increase in the scoring function $S(y^t, x)$.

Let $(c_i^* \dots c_j^*)$ be the set of constants "merged" by setting their AREEQUAL predicate to true. The EXPANDPREDICATES procedure creates new predicates AREEQUAL$(c_i^* \dots c_j^*, c_k \dots c_l)$ corresponding to all the potential predicates created by merging the constants $c_i^* \dots c_j^*$ with any of the other previously merged constants. For example, after the first iteration, a pair of constants (c_i^*, c_j^*) are merged. The set of predicates are expanded to include AREEQUAL(c_i^*, c_j^*, c_k) $\forall c_k$, reflecting all possible additional references to the proposed object referenced by c_i^*, c_j^*.

This algorithm continues until there is no predicate that can be set to true that increases the score function.

In this way, the final setting of F_y is a local maximum of the score function. As in other search algorithms, we can employ look-ahead to reduce the greediness of the search (i.e., consider multiple merges simultaneously), although we do not include look-ahead in experiments reported here.

It is important to note that each expansion of the aggregate query predicates F_y has a corresponding set of aggregate *evidence* predicates. These evidence predicates characterize the compatibility of the attributes of each hypothesized object.

3.4.1 Pruning

The space required for the above algorithm scales $\Omega(|C|^2)$, since in the initialization step we must ground a predicate for each pair of constants. We use the *canopy method* of McCallum et al. (2000), which thresholds a "cheap" similarity metric to prune unnecessary comparisons. This pruning can be done at subsequent stages of inference to restrict which predicates variables will be introduced.

Additionally, we must ensure that predicate settings at time t do not contradict settings at $t-1$ (e.g. if $F^t(a,b,c)=1$, then $F^{t+1}(a,b)=1$). By greedily setting unobserved nodes to their MAP estimates, the inference algorithm ignores inconsistent settings and removes them from the search space.

3.5 Parameter estimation

Given a fully labeled training set $\mathcal{D}$ of constants annotated with their referent objects, we would like to estimate the value of w that maximizes the likelihood of $\mathcal{D}$. That is, $w^* = \text{argmax}_w P_w(y|x)$.

When the data are few, we can explicitly instantiate all AREEQUAL($\mathbf{d}$) predicates, setting their corresponding nodes to the values implied by $\mathcal{D}$. The likelihood is given by Equation 1, where the normalizer is $Z_{\mathbf{x}} = \sum_{y'} \exp\left(\sum_{i=1}^{|F'_y|} w_i n_i(x,y')\right)$.

Although this sum over y' to calculate $Z_{\mathbf{x}}$ is exponential in $|\mathbf{y}|$, many inconsistent settings can be pruned as discussed in Section 3.4.1.

In general, however, instantiating the entire set of predicates denoted by y and calculating $Z_{\mathbf{x}}$ is intractable. Existing methods for MLN parameter estimation include pseudo-likelihood and voted perceptron (Richardson and Domingos, 2004; Singla and Domingos, 2005). We instead follow the recent success in *piecewise training* for complex undirected graphical models (Sutton and McCallum, 2005) by making the following two approximations. First, we avoid calculating the global normalizer $Z_{\mathbf{x}}$ by calculating local normalizers, which sum only over the two values for each aggregate query predicate *grounded in the training data*. We therefore maximize the sum of *local* probabilities for each query predicate given the evidence predicates.

This approximation can be viewed as constructing a log-linear binary classifier to predict whether an isolated set of constants refer to the same object. Input features include arbitrary first-order features over the input constants, and the output is a binary variable. The parameters of this classifier correspond to the w weights in the MLN. This simplification results in a convex optimization problem, which we solve using gradient descent with L-BFGS, a second-order optimization method (Liu and Nocedal, 1989).

The second approximation addresses the fact that all query predicates from the training set cannot be instantiated. We instead sample a subset $F_S \in F_y$ and maximize the likelihood of this subset. The sampling is not strictly uniform, but is instead obtained by collecting the predicates created while performing object identification using a weak method (e.g. string comparisons). More explicitly, predicates are sampled from the training data by performing greedy agglomerative clustering on the training mentions, using a scoring function that computes the similarity between two nodes by string edit distance. The goal of this clustering is not to exactly reproduce the training clusters, but to generate correct and incorrect clusters that have similar characteristics (size, homogeneity) to what will be present in the testing data.

4 Experiments

We perform experiments on two object identification tasks: *citation matching* and *author disambiguation*. *Citation matching* is the task of determining whether two research paper citation strings refer to the same paper. We use the Citeseer corpus (Lawrence et al., 1999), containing approximately 1500 citations, 900 of which are unique. The citations are manually labeled with cluster identifiers, and the strings are segmented into fields such as author, title, etc. The citation data is split into four disjoint categories by topic, and the results presented are obtained by training on three categories and testing on the fourth.

Using first-order logic, we create a number of aggregate predicates such as ALLTITLESMATCH, ALLAUTHORSMATCH, ALLJOURNALSMATCH, etc., as well as their existential counterparts, THEREEXISTSTITLEMATCH, etc. We also include *count* predicates, which indicate the number of these matches in a set of constants.

Additionally, we add edit distance predicates, which calculate approximate matches[1] between title fields, etc., for each pair of citations in a set of citations. Aggregate features are used for these, such as "there exists a pair of citations in this cluster which have titles that are less than 30% similar" and "the minimum edit distance between titles in a cluster is greater than 50%."

We evaluate using pairwise precision, recall, and F1, which measure the system's ability to predict whether each pair of constants refer to the same object or not. Table 1 shows the advantage of our

[1]We use the Secondstring package, found at http://secondstring.sourceforge.net

Table 1: Precision, recall, and F1 performance for citation matching task, where OBJECTS is an MLN using aggregate predicates, and PAIRS is an MLN using only pairwise predicates. OBJECTS outperforms PAIRS on three of the four testing sets.

	Objects			Pairs		
	pr	re	f1	pr	re	f1
constraint	85.8	79.1	**82.3**	63.0	98.0	76.7
reinforce	97.0	90.0	**93.4**	65.6	98.2	78.7
face	93.4	84.8	**88.9**	74.2	94.7	83.2
reason	97.4	69.3	81.0	76.4	95.5	**84.9**

Table 2: Performance on the author disambiguation task. OBJECTS outperforms PAIRS on two of the three testing sets.

	Objects			Pairs		
	pr	re	f1	pr	re	f1
miller d	73.9	29.3	41.9	44.6	1.0	**61.7**
li w	39.4	47.9	**43.2**	22.1	1.0	36.2
smith b	61.2	70.1	**65.4**	14.5	1.0	25.4

proposed model (OBJECTS) over a model that only considers pairwise predicates of the same features (PAIRS). Note that PAIRS is a strong baseline that performs collective inference of citation matching decisions, but is restricted to use only ISEQUAL(c_i, c_j) predicates over pairs of citations. Thus, the performance difference is due to the ability to model first-order features of the data.

Author disambiguation is the task of deciding whether two strings refer to the same author. To increase the task complexity, we collect citations from the Web containing different authors with matching last names and first initials. Thus, simply performing a string match on the author's name would be insufficient in many cases. We searched for three common last name / first initial combinations (MILLER, D; LI, W; SMITH, B). From this set, we collected 400 citations referring to 56 unique authors. For these experiments, we train on two subsets and test on the third.

We generate aggregate predicates similar to those used for citation matching. Additionally, we include features indicating the overlap of tokens from the titles and indicating whether there exists a pair of authors in this cluster that have different middle names. This last feature exemplifies the sort of reasoning enabled by aggregate predicates: For example, consider a pairwise predicate that indicates whether two authors have the same middle name. Very often, middle name information is unavailable, so the name "Miller, A." may have high similarity to both "Miller, A. B." and "Miller, A. C.". However, it is unlikely that the same person has two different middle names, and our model learns a weight for this feature. Table 2 demonstrates the advantage of this method.

Overall, OBJECTS achieves $F1$ scores superior to PAIRS on 5 of the 7 datasets. These results indicate the potential advantages of using complex first-order quantifiers in MLNs. The cases in which PAIRS outperforms OBJECTS are likely due to the fact that the approximate inference used in OBJECTS is greedy. Increasing the robustness of inference is a topic of future research.

5 Conclusions and Future Work

We have presented an algorithm that enables practical inference in MLNs containing first-order existential and universal quantifiers, and have demonstrated the advantages of this approach on two real-world datasets. Future work will investigate efficient ways to improve the approximations made during inference, for example by reducing its greediness by revising the MAP estimates made at previous iterations.

Although the optimal number of objects is chosen implicitly by the inference algorithm, there may be reasons to explicitly model this number. For example, if there exist global features of the data that suggest there are many objects, then the inference algorithm should be less inclined to merge constants. Additionally, the data may exhibit "preferential attachment" such that the probability of a constant being added to an existing object is proportional to the number of constants that refer to that object. Future work will examine the feasibility of adding aggregate query predicates to represent these values.

More subtly, one may also want to directly model the size of the object population. For example, given a database of authors, we may want to estimate not only how many distinct authors exist in the database, but also how many distinct authors exist outside of the database, as discussed in Milch et al. (2005). Discriminatively-trained models cannot easily reason about objects for which they have no observations; so a generative/discriminative hybrid model may be required to properly estimate this value.

Finally, while the inference algorithm we describe is evaluated only on the object uncertainty task, we would like to extend it to perform inference over arbitrary query predicates.

6 Acknowledgments

We would like to thank the reviewers, and Pallika Kanani for helpful discussions. This work was supported in part by the Center for Intelligent Information Retrieval, in part by U.S. Government contract #NBCH040171 through a subcontract with BBNT Solutions LLC, in part by The Central Intelligence Agency, the National Security Agency and National Science Foundation under NSF grant #IIS-0326249, and in part by the Defense Advanced Research Projects Agency (DARPA), through the Department of the Interior, NBC, Acquisition Services Division, under contract number NBCHD030010. Any opinions, findings and conclusions or recommendations expressed in this material are the author(s)' and do not necessarily reflect those of the sponsor.

References

Nikhil Bansal, Avrim Blum, and Shuchi Chawla. 2004. Correlation clustering. *Machine Learining*, 56:89–113.

Yuri Boykov, Olga Veksler, and Ramin Zabih. 2001. Fast approximate energy minimization via graph cuts. *In IEEE transactions on Pattern Analysis and Machine Intelligence (PAMI)*, 23(11):1222–1239.

Peter Carbonetto, Jacek Kisynski, Nando de Freitas, and David Poole. 2005. Nonparametric bayesian logic. In *UAI*.

J. Cussens. 2003. Individuals, relations and structures in probabilistic models. In *Proceedings of the Fifteenth Conference on Uncertainty in Artificial Intelligence*, pages 126–133, Acapulco, Mexico.

Hal Daumé III and Daniel Marcu. 2004. Supervised clustering with the dirichlet process. In *NIPS'04 Learning With Structured Outputs Workshop*, Whistler, Canada.

Rodrigo de Salvo Braz, Eyal Amir, and Dan Roth. 2005. Lifted first-order probabilistic inference. In *IJCAI*, pages 1319–1325.

L. Dehaspe. 1997. Maximum entropy modeling with clausal constraints. In *Proceedings of the Seventh International Workshop on Inductive Logic Programming*, pages 109–125, Prague, Czech Republic.

I. P. Fellegi and A. B. Sunter. 1969. A theory for record linkage. *Journal of the American Statistical Association*, 64:1183–1210.

Nir Friedman, Lise Getoor, Daphne Koller, and Avi Pfeffer. 1999. Learning probabilistic relational models. In *IJCAI*, pages 1300–1309.

John Lafferty, Andrew McCallum, and Fernando Pereira. 2001. Conditional random fields: Probabilistic models for segmenting and labeling sequence data. In *Proc. 18th International Conf. on Machine Learning*, pages 282–289. Morgan Kaufmann, San Francisco, CA.

S. Lawrence, C. L. Giles, and K. Bollaker. 1999. Digital libraries and autonomous citation indexing. *IEEE Computer*, 32:67–71.

D. C. Liu and J. Nocedal. 1989. On the limited memory BFGS method for large scale optimization. *Math. Programming*, 45(3, (Ser. B)):503–528.

A. McCallum and B. Wellner. 2003. Toward conditional models of identity uncertainty with application to proper noun coreference. In *IJCAI Workshop on Information Integration on the Web*.

Andrew K. McCallum, Kamal Nigam, and Lyle Ungar. 2000. Efficient clustering of high-dimensional data sets with application to reference matching. In *Proceedings of the Sixth International Conference On Knowledge Discovery and Data Mining (KDD-2000)*, Boston, MA.

Joseph F. McCarthy and Wendy G. Lehnert. 1995. Using decision trees for coreference resolution. In *IJCAI*, pages 1050–1055.

Brian Milch, Bhaskara Marthi, and Stuart Russell. 2004. Blog: Relational modeling with unknown objects. In *ICML 2004 Workshop on Statistical Relational Learning and Its Connections to Other Fields*.

Brian Milch, Bhaskara Marthi, and Stuart Russell. 2005. BLOG: Probabilistic models with unknown objects. In *IJCAI*.

Parag and Pedro Domingos. 2004. Multi-relational record linkage. In *Proceedings of the KDD-2004 Workshop on Multi-Relational Data Mining*, pages 31–48, August.

D. Poole. 2003. First-order probabilistic inference. In *Proceedings of the Eighteenth International Joint Conference on Artificial Intelligence*, pages 985–991, Acapulco, Mexico. Morgan Kaufman.

M. Richardson and P. Domingos. 2004. Markov logic networks. Technical report, University of Washington, Seattle, WA.

Parag Singla and Pedro Domingos. 2005. Discriminative training of markov logic networks. In *Proceedings of the Twentieth National Conference of Artificial Intelligence*, Pittsburgh, PA.

Wee Meng Soon, Hwee Tou Ng, and Daniel Chung Yong Lim. 2001. A machine learning approach to coreference resolution of noun phrases. *Comput. Linguist.*, 27(4):521–544.

Charles Sutton and Andrew McCallum. 2005. Piecewise training of undirected models. In *Submitted to 21st Conference on Uncertainty in Artificial Intelligence*.

Ben Taskar, Abbeel Pieter, and Daphne Koller. 2002. Discriminative probabilistic models for relational data. In *Uncertainty in Artificial Intelligence: Proceedings of the Eighteenth Conference (UAI-2002)*, pages 485–492, San Francisco, CA. Morgan Kaufmann Publishers.

William E. Winkler. 1993. Improved decision rules in the fellegi-sunter model of record linkage. Technical report, Statistical Research Division, U.S. Census Bureau, Washington, DC.

Re-Ranking Algorithms for Name Tagging

Heng Ji
Dept. of Computer Science

Cynthia Rudin
Center for Neural Science and Courant Institute of Mathematical Sciences

Ralph Grishman
Dept. of Computer Science

New York University
New York, N.Y. 10003

hengji@cs.nyu.edu rudin@nyu.edu grishman@cs.nyu.edu

Abstract

Integrating information from different stages of an NLP processing pipeline can yield significant error reduction. We demonstrate how re-ranking can improve name tagging in a Chinese information extraction system by incorporating information from relation extraction, event extraction, and coreference. We evaluate three state-of-the-art re-ranking algorithms (MaxEnt-Rank, SVMRank, and p-Norm Push Ranking), and show the benefit of multi-stage re-ranking for cross-sentence and cross-document inference.

1 Introduction

In recent years, re-ranking techniques have been successfully applied to enhance the performance of NLP analysis components based on generative models. A baseline generative model produces N-best candidates, which are then re-ranked using a rich set of local and global features in order to select the best analysis. Various supervised learning algorithms have been adapted to the task of re-ranking for NLP systems, such as MaxEnt-Rank (Charniak and Johnson, 2005; Ji and Grishman, 2005), SVMRank (Shen and Joshi, 2003), Voted Perceptron (Collins, 2002; Collins and Duffy, 2002; Shen and Joshi, 2004), Kernel Based Methods (Henderson and Titov, 2005), and RankBoost (Collins, 2002; Collins and Koo, 2003; Kudo et al., 2005).

These algorithms have been used primarily within the context of a single NLP analysis component, with the most intensive study devoted to improving parsing performance. The re-ranking models for parsing, for example, normally rely on structures generated within the baseline parser itself. Achieving really high performance for some analysis components, however, requires that we take a broader view, one that looks outside a single component in order to bring to bear knowledge from the entire NL analysis process. In this paper we will demonstrate the potential of this approach in enhancing the performance of Chinese name tagging within an information extraction application.

Combining information from other stages in the analysis pipeline allows us to incorporate information from a much wider context, spanning the entire document and even going across documents. This will give rise to new design issues; we will examine and compare different re-ranking algorithms when applied to this task.

We shall first describe the general setting and the special characteristics of re-ranking for name tagging. Then we present and evaluate three re-ranking algorithms – MaxEnt-Rank, SVMRank and a new algorithm, p-Norm Push Ranking – for this problem, and show how an approach based on multi-stage re-ranking can effectively handle features across sentence and document boundaries.

2 Prior Work

2.1 Ranking

We will describe the three state-of-the-art supervised ranking techniques considered in this work. Later we shall apply and evaluate these algorithms for re-ranking in the context of name tagging.

Maximum Entropy modeling (MaxEnt) has been extremely successful for many NLP classifi-

Workshop on Computationally Hard Problemsand Joint Inference in Speech and Language Processing, pages 49–56,
New York City, New York, June 2006.

cation tasks, so it is natural to apply it to re-ranking problems. (Charniak and Johnson, 2005) applied MaxEnt to improve the performance of a state-of-art parser; also in (Ji and Grishman, 2005) we used it to improve a Chinese name tagger.

Using SVMRank, (Shen and Joshi, 2003) achieved significant improvement on parse re-ranking. They compared two different sample creation methods, and presented an efficient training method by separating the training samples into subsets.

The last approach we consider is a boosting-style approach. We implement a new algorithm called p-Norm Push Ranking (Rudin, 2006). This algorithm is a generalization of RankBoost (Freund et al. 1998) which concentrates specifically on the top portion of a ranked list. The parameter "p" determines how much the algorithm concentrates at the top.

2.2 Enhancing Named Entity Taggers

There have been a very large number of NE tagger implementations since this task was introduced at MUC-6 (Grishman and Sundheim, 1996). Most implementations use local features and a unifying learning algorithm based on, e.g., an HMM, MaxEnt, or SVM. Collins (2002) augmented a baseline NE tagger with a re-ranker that used only local, NE-oriented features. Roth and Yih (2002) combined NE and semantic relation tagging, but within a quite different framework (using a linear programming model for joint inference).

3 A Framework for Name Re-Ranking

3.1 The Information Extraction Pipeline

The extraction task we are addressing is that of the Automatic Content Extraction (ACE)[1] evaluations. The 2005 ACE evaluation had 7 types of entities, of which the most common were PER (persons), ORG (organizations), LOC (natural locations) and GPE ('geo-political entities' – locations which are also political units, such as countries, counties, and cities). There were 6 types of semantic relations, with 18 subtypes. Examples of these relations are "the CEO of Microsoft" (an *organization-affiliation* relation), "Fred's wife" (a *personal-social* relation), and "a military base in Germany" (a *located* relation). And there were 8 types of events, with 33 subtypes, such as "Kurt Schork died in Sierra Leone yesterday" (a *Die* event), and "Schweitzer founded a hospital in 1913" (a *Start-Org* event).

To extract these elements we have developed a Chinese information extraction pipeline that consists of the following stages:

- Name tagging and name structure parsing (which identifies the internal structure of some names);
- Coreference resolution, which links "mentions" (referring phrases of selected semantic types) into "entities": this stage is a combination of high-precision heuristic rules and maximum entropy models;
- Relation tagging, using a K-nearest-neighbor algorithm to identify relation types and subtypes;
- Event patterns, semi-automatically extracted from ACE training corpora.

3.2 Hypothesis Representation and Generation

Again, the central idea is to apply the baseline name tagger to generate N-Best multiple hypotheses for each sentence; the results from subsequent components are then exploited to re-rank these hypotheses and the new top hypothesis is output as the final result.

In our name re-ranking model, each hypothesis is an NE tagging of *the entire sentence*. For example, "`<PER>John</PER> was born in <GPE>New York</GPE>.`" is one hypothesis for the sentence "John was born in New York".

We apply a HMM tagger to identify four named entity types: Person, GPE, Organization and Location. The HMM tagger generally follows the Nymble model (Bikel et al, 1997), and uses best-first search to generate N-Best hypotheses. It also computes the "margin", which is the difference between the log probabilities of the top two hypotheses. This is used as a rough measure of confidence in the top hypothesis. A large margin indicates greater confidence that the first hypothesis is correct. The margin also determines the number of hypotheses (N) that we will store. Using cross-validation on the training data, we determine the value of N required to include the best

[1] The ACE task description can be found at http://www.itl.nist.gov/iad/894.01/tests/ace/

hypothesis, as a function of the margin. We then divide the margin into ranges of values, and set a value of N for each range, with a maximum of 30.

To obtain the training data for the re-ranking algorithm, we separate the name tagging training corpus into k folders, and train the HMM name tagger on k-1 folders. We then use the HMM to generate N-Best hypotheses $H = \{h_1, h_2, ..., h_N\}$ for each sentence in the remaining folder. Each h_i in H is then paired with its NE F-measure, measured against the key in the annotated corpus.

We define a "crucial pair" as a pair of hypotheses such that, according to F-Measure, the first hypothesis in the pair should be more highly ranked than the second. That is, if for a sentence, the F-Measure of hypothesis h_i is larger than that of h_j, then (h_i, h_j) is a crucial pair.

3.3 Re-Ranking Functions

We investigated the following three different formulations of the re-ranking problem:

- Direct Re-Ranking by Score
For each hypothesis h_i, we attempt to learn a scoring function $f : H \rightarrow R$, such that $f(h_i) > f(h_j)$ if the F-Measure of h_i is higher than the F-measure of h_j.

- Direct Re-Ranking by Classification
For each hypothesis h_i, we attempt to learn $f : H \rightarrow \{-1, 1\}$, such that $f(h_i) = 1$ if h_i has the top F-Measure among H; otherwise $f(h_i) = -1$. This can be considered a special case of re-ranking by score.

- Indirect Re-Ranking Function
For each "crucial" pair of hypotheses (h_i, h_j), we learn $f : H \times H \rightarrow \{-1, 1\}$, such that $f(h_i, h_j) = 1$ if h_i is better than h_j; $f(h_i, h_j) = -1$ if h_i is worse than h_j. We call this "indirect" ranking because we need to apply an additional decoding step to pick the best hypothesis from these pair-wise comparison results.

4 Features for Re-Ranking

4.1 Inferences From Subsequent Stages

Information extraction is a potentially symbiotic pipeline with strong dependencies between stages (Roth and Yih, 2002&2004; Ji and Grishman, 2005). Thus, we use features based on the output of four subsequent stages – name structure parsing, relation extraction, event patterns, and coreference analysis – to seek the best hypothesis.

We included ten features based on name structure parsing to capture the local information missed by the baseline name tagger such as details of the structure of Chinese person names.

The relation and event re-ranking features are based on matching patterns of words or constituents. They serve to correct name boundary errors (because such errors would prevent some patterns from matching). They also exert selectional preferences on their arguments, and so serve to correct name type errors. For each relation argument, we included a feature whose value is the likelihood that relation appears with an argument of that semantic type (these probabilities are obtained from the training corpus and binned). For each event pattern, a feature records whether the types of the arguments match those required by the pattern.

Coreference can link multiple mentions of names provided they have the same spelling (though if a name has several parts, some may be dropped) and same semantic type. So if the boundary or type of one mention can be determined with some confidence, coreference can be used to disambiguate other mentions, by favoring hypotheses which support more coreference. To this end, we incorporate several features based on coreference, such as the number of mentions referring to a name candidate.

Each of these features is defined for individual name candidates; the value of the feature for a hypothesis is the sum of its values over all names in the hypothesis. The complete set of detailed features is listed in (Ji and Grishman, 2006).

4.2 Handling Cross-Sentence Features by Multi-Stage Re-Ranking

Coreference is potentially a powerful contributor for enhancing NE recognition, because it provides information from other sentences and even documents, and it applies to all sentences that include names. For a name candidate, 62% of its coreference relations span sentence boundaries. However, this breadth poses a problem because it means that the score of a hypothesis for a given sentence may depend on the tags assigned to the same names in other sentences.[2]

Ideally, when we re-rank the hypotheses for one sentence *S*, the other sentences that include mentions of the same name should already have been re-ranked, but this is not possible because of the mutual dependence. Repeated re-ranking of a sentence would be time-consuming, so we have adopted an alternative approach. Instead of incorporating coreference evidence with all other information in one re-ranker, we apply two re-rankers in succession.

In the first re-ranking step, we generate new rankings for all sentences based on name structure, relation and event features, which are all sentence-internal evidence. Then in a second pass, we apply a re-ranker based on coreference between the names in each hypothesis of sentence *S* and the mentions in the top-ranking hypothesis (from the first re-ranker) of all other sentences.[3] In this way, the coreference re-ranker can propagate globally (across sentences and documents) high-confidence decisions based on the other evidence. In our final MaxEnt Ranker we obtained a small additional gain by further splitting the first re-ranker into three separate steps: a name structure based re-ranker, a relation based re-ranker and an event based re-ranker; these were incorporated in an incremental structure.

4.3 Adding Cross-Document Information

The idea in coreference is to link a name mention whose tag is locally ambiguous to another mention that is unambiguously tagged based on local evidence. The wider a net we can cast, the greater the chance of success. To cast the widest net possible, we have used cross-document coreference for the test set. We cluster the documents using a cross-entropy metric and then treat the entire cluster as a single document.

We take all the name candidates in the top *N* hypotheses for each sentence in each cluster *T* to construct a "query set" *Q*. The metric used for the clustering is the cross entropy *H(T, d)* between the distribution of the name candidates in *T* and document *d*. If *H(T, d)* is smaller than a threshold then we add *d* to *T*. *H(T, d)* is defined by:

$$H(T,d) = -\sum_{x \in Q} prob(T,x) \times \log prob(d,x).$$

We built these clusters two ways: first, just clustering the test documents; second, by augmenting these clusters with related documents retrieved from a large unlabeled corpus (with document relevance measured using cross-entropy).

5 Re-Ranking Algorithms

We have been focusing on selecting appropriate ranking algorithms to fit our application. We choose three state-of-the-art ranking algorithms that have good generalization ability. We now describe these algorithms.

5.1 MaxEnt-Rank

5.1.1 Sampling and Pruning

Maximum Entropy models are useful for the task of ranking because they compute a reliable ranking probability for each hypothesis. We have tried two different sampling methods – single sampling and pairwise sampling.

The first approach is to use each single hypothesis h_i as a sample. Only the best hypothesis of each sentence is regarded as a positive sample; all the rest are regarded as negative samples. In general, absolute values of features are not good indicators of whether a hypothesis will be the best hypothesis for a sentence; for example, a coreferring mention count of 7 may be excellent for one sentence and poor for another. Consequently, in this single-hypothesis-sampling approach, we convert each feature to a Boolean value, which is true if the original feature takes on its maximum value (among all hypotheses) for this hypothesis. This does, however, lose some of the detail about the differences between hypotheses.

In pairwise sampling we used each pair of hypotheses (h_i, h_j) as a sample. The value of a feature for a sample is the difference between its values for the two hypotheses. However, considering all pairs causes the number of samples to grow quadratically ($O(N^2)$) with the number of hypotheses, compared to the linear growth with best/non-best sampling. To make the training and

2 For in-document coreference, this problem could be avoided if the tagging of an entire document constituted a hypothesis, but that would be impractical … a very large N would be required to capture sufficient alternative taggings in an N-best framework.

3 This second pass is skipped for sentences for which the confidence in the top hypothesis produced by the first re-ranker is above a threshold.

test procedures more efficient, we prune the data in several ways.

We perform pruning by beam setting, removing candidate hypotheses that possess very low probabilities from the HMM, and during training we discard the hypotheses with very low F-measure scores. Additionally, we incorporate the pruning techniques used in (Chiang 2005), by which any hypothesis with a probability lower than α times the highest probability for one sentence is discarded. We also discard the pairs very close in performance or probability.

5.1.2 Decoding

If f is the ranking function, the MaxEnt model produces a probability for each un-pruned "crucial" pair: $prob(f(h_i, h_j) = 1)$, i.e., the probability that for the given sentence, h_i is a better hypothesis than h_j. We need an additional decoding step to select the best hypothesis. Inspired by the caching idea and the multi-class solution proposed by (Platt et al. 2000), we use a dynamic decoding algorithm with complexity O(n) as follows.

We scale the probability values into three types: CompareResult (h_i, h_j) = "better" if $prob(f(h_i, h_j) = 1) > \delta_1$, "worse" if $prob(f(h_i, h_j) = 1) < \delta_2$, and "unsure" otherwise, where $\delta_1 \geqslant \delta_2$.[4]

Prune

```
for i = 1 to n
   Num = 0;
   for j = 1 to n and j≠i
        If CompareResult(hi, hj) = "worse"
            Num++;
   if Num> β then discard hi from H
```

Select

```
Initialize: i = 1, j = n
while (i<j)
    if CompareResult(hi, hj) = "better"
       discard hj from H;
       j--;
    else if CompareResult(hi, hj) = "worse"
       discard hi from H;
       i++;
    else break;
```

Output

If the number of remaining hypotheses in H is 1, then output it as the best hypothesis; else propagate all hypothesis pairs into the next re-ranker.

5.2 SVMRank

We implemented an SVM-based model, which can theoretically achieve very low generalization error. We use the SVMLight package (Joachims, 1998), with the pairwise sampling scheme as for MaxEnt-Rank. In addition we made the following adaptations: we calibrated the SVM outputs, and separated the data into subsets.

To speed up training, we divided our training samples into k subsets. Each subset contains $N(N-1)/k$ pairs of hypotheses of each sentence.

In order to combine the results from these different SVMs, we must calibrate the function values; the output of an SVM yields a distance to the separating hyperplane, but not a probability. We have applied the method described in (Shen and Joshi, 2003), to map SVM's results to probabilities via a sigmoid. Thus from the kth SVM, we get the probability for each pair of hypotheses:

$$prob(f_k(h_i, h_j) = 1),$$

namely the probability of h_i being better than h_j. Then combining all k SVMs' results we get:

$$Z(h_i, h_j) = \prod_k prob(f_k(h_i, h_j) = 1).$$

So the hypothesis h_i with maximal value is chosen as the top hypothesis:

$$\arg\max_{h_i}(\prod_j Z(h_i, h_j)).$$

5.3 P-Norm Push Ranking

The third algorithm we have tried is a general boosting-style supervised ranking algorithm called p-Norm Push Ranking (Rudin, 2006). We describe this algorithm in more detail since it is quite new and we do not expect many readers to be familiar with it.

The parameter "p" determines how much emphasis (or "push") is placed closer to the top of the ranked list, where p≥1. The p-Norm Push Ranking algorithm generalizes RankBoost (take p=1 for RankBoost). When p is set at a large value, the rankings at the top of the list are given higher priority (a large "push"), at the expense of possibly making misranks towards the bottom of the list.

[4] In the final stage re-ranker we use $\delta_1 = \delta_2$ so that we don't generate the output of "unsure", and one hypothesis is finally selected.

Since for our application, we do not care about the rankings at the bottom of the list (i.e., we do not care about the exact rank ordering of the bad hypotheses), this algorithm is suitable for our problem. There is a tradeoff for the choice of p; larger p yields more accurate results at the very top of the list for the training data. If we want to consider more than simply the very top of the list, we may desire a smaller value of p. Note that larger values of p also require more training data in order to maintain generalization ability (as shown both by theoretical generalization bounds and experiments). If we want large p, we must aim to choose the largest value of p that allows generalization, given our amount of training data. When we are working on the first stage of re-ranking, we consider the whole top portion of the ranked list, because we use the rank in the list as a feature for the next stage. Thus, we have chosen the value p_1=4 (a small "push") for the first re-ranker. For the second re-ranker we choose p_2=16 (a large "push").

The objective of the p-Norm Push Ranking algorithm is to create a scoring function $f: H \rightarrow R$ such that for each crucial pair (h_i, h_j), we shall have $f(h_i) > f(h_j)$. The form of the scoring function is $f(h_i) = \sum \alpha_k g_k(h_i)$, where g_k is called a weak ranker: $g_k : H \rightarrow [0,1]$. The values of α_k are determined by the p-Norm Push algorithm in an iterative way.

The weak rankers g_k are the features described in Section 4. Note that we sometimes allow the algorithm to use both g_k and $g'_k(h_i)=1-g_k(h_i)$ as weak rankers, namely when g_k has low accuracy on the training set; this way the algorithm itself can decide which to use.

As in the style of boosting algorithms, real-valued weights are placed on each of the training crucial pairs, and these weights are successively updated by the algorithm. Higher weights are given to those crucial pairs that were misranked at the previous iteration, especially taking into account the pairs near the top of the list. At each iteration, one weak ranker g_k is chosen by the algorithm, based on the weights. The coefficient α_k is then updated accordingly.

6 Experiment Results

6.1 Data and Resources

We use 100 texts from the ACE 04 training corpus for a blind test. The test set included 2813 names: 1126 persons, 712 GPEs, 785 organizations and 190 locations. The performance is measured via Precision (P), Recall (R) and F-Measure (F).

The baseline name tagger is trained from 2978 texts from the People's Daily news in 1998 and also 1300 texts from ACE training data.

The 1,071,285 training samples (pairs of hypotheses) for the re-rankers are obtained from the name tagger applied on the ACE training data, in the manner described in Section 3.2.

We use OpenNLP[5] for the MaxEnt-Rank experiments. We use SVM^{light} (Joachims, 1998) for SVMRank, with a linear kernel and the soft margin parameter set to the default value. For the p-Norm Push Ranking, we apply 33 weak rankers, i.e., features described in Section 4. The number of iterations was fixed at 110, this number was chosen by optimizing the performance on a development set of 100 documents.

6.2 Effect of Pairwise Sampling

We have tried both single-hypothesis and pairwise sampling (described in section 5.1.1) in MaxEnt-Rank and p-Norm Push Ranking. Table 1 shows that pairwise sampling helps both algorithms. MaxEnt-Rank benefited more from it, with precision and recall increased 2.2% and 0.4% respectively.

Model		P	R	F
MaxEnt-Rank	Single Sampling	89.6	90.2	89.9
	Pairwise Sampling	91.8	90.6	91.2
p-Norm Push	Single Sampling	91.4	89.6	90.5
	Pairwise Sampling	91.2	90.8	91.0

Table 1. Effect of Pairwise Sampling

6.3 Overall Performance

In Table 2 we report the overall performance for these three algorithms. All of them achieved improvements on the baseline name tagger. MaxEnt yields the highest precision, while p-Norm Push Ranking with p_2 = 16 yields the highest recall.

A larger value of "p" encourages the p-Norm Push Ranking algorithm to perform better near the top of the ranked list. As we discussed in section

[5] http://maxent.sourceforge.net/index.html

5.3, we use $p_1 = 4$ (a small "push") for the first re-ranker and $p_2 = 16$ (a big "push") for the second re-ranker. From Table 2 we can see that $p_2 = 16$ obviously performed better than $p_2 = 1$. In general, we have observed that for $p_2 \leqslant 16$, larger p_2 correlates with better results.

Model	P	R	F
Baseline	87.4	87.6	87.5
MaxEnt-Rank	91.8	90.6	91.2
SVMRank	89.5	90.1	89.8
p-Norm Push Ranking (p_2=16)	91.2	90.8	91.0
p-Norm Push Ranking (p_2=1, RankBoost)	89.3	89.7	89.5

Table 2. Overall Performance

The improved NE results brought better performance for the subsequent stages of information extraction too. We use the NE outputs from MaxEnt-Ranker as inputs for coreference resolver and relation tagger. The ACE value[6] of entity detection (mention detection + coreference resolution) is increased from 73.2 to 76.5; the ACE value of relation detection is increased from 34.2 to 34.8.

6.4 Effect of Cross-document Information

As described in Section 4.3, our algorithm incorporates cross-document coreference information. The 100 texts in the test set were first clustered into 28 topics (clusters). We then apply cross-document coreference on each cluster. Compared to single document coreference, cross-document coreference obtained 0.5% higher F-Measure, using MaxEnt-Ranker, improving performance for 15 of these 28 clusters.

These clusters were then extended by selecting 84 additional related texts from a corpus of 15,000 unlabeled Chinese news articles (using a cross-entropy metric to select texts). 24 clusters gave further improvement, and an overall 0.2% further improvement on F-Measure was obtained.

6.5 Efficiency

Model	Training	Test
MaxEnt-Rank	7 hours	55 minutes
SVMRank	48 hours	2 hours
p-Norm Push Ranking	3.2 hours	10 minutes

Table 3. Efficiency Comparison

In Table 3 we summarize the running time of these three algorithms in our application.

7 Discussion

We have shown that the other components of an IE pipeline can provide information which can substantially improve the performance of an NE tagger, and that these improvements can be realized through a variety of re-ranking algorithms. MaxEnt re-ranking using binary sampling and p-Norm Push Ranking proved about equally effective.[7] p-Norm Push Ranking was particularly efficient for decoding (about 10 documents / minute), although no great effort was invested in tuning these procedures for speed.

We presented methods to handle cross-sentence inference using staged re-ranking and to incorporate additional evidence through document clustering.

An N-best / re-ranking strategy has proven effective for this task because with relatively small values of N we are already able to include highly-rated hypotheses for most sentences. Using the values of N we have used throughout (dependent on the margin of the baseline HMM, but never above 30), the upper bound of N-best performance (if we always picked the top-scoring hypothesis) is 97.4% recall, 96.2% precision, F=96.8%.

Collins (2002) also applied re-ranking to improve name tagging. Our work has addressed both name identification and classification, while his only evaluated name identification. Our re-ranker used features from other pipeline stages, while his were limited to local features involving lexical information and 'word-shape' in a 5-token window. Since these feature sets are essentially disjoint, it is quite possible that a combination of the two could yield even further improvements. His boosting algorithm is a modification of the method in (Freund et al., 1998), an adaptation of AdaBoost, whereas our p-Norm Push Ranking algorithm can emphasize the hypotheses near the top, matching our objective.

Roth and Yih (2004) combined information from named entities and semantic relation tagging, adopting a similar overall goal but using a quite different approach based on linear programming.

[6] The ACE04 value scoring metric can be found at: http://www.nist.gov/speech/tests/ace/ace04/doc/ace04-evalplan-v7.pdf

[7] The features were initially developed and tested using the MaxEnt re-ranker, so it is encouraging that they worked equally well with the p-Norm Push Ranker without further tuning.

They limited themselves to name classification, assuming the identification given. This may be a natural subtask for English, where capitalization is a strong indicator of a name, but is much less useful for Chinese, where there is no capitalization or word segmentation, and boundary errors on name identification are frequent. Expanding their approach to cover identification would have greatly increased the number of hypotheses and made their approach slower. In contrast, we adjust the number of hypotheses based on the margin in order to maintain efficiency while minimizing the chance of losing a high-quality hypothesis.

In addition we were able to capture selectional preferences (probabilities of semantic types as arguments of particular semantic relations as computed from the corpus), whereas Roth and Yih limited themselves to hard (boolean) type constraints.

Acknowledgment

This material is based upon work supported by the Defense Advanced Research Projects Agency under Contract No. HR0011-06-C-0023, and the National Science Foundation under Grant IIS-00325657 and a postdoctoral research fellowship. Any opinions, findings and conclusions expressed in this material are those of the authors and do not necessarily reflect the views of the U. S. Government.

References

Daniel M. Bikel, Scott Miller, Richard Schwartz, and Ralph Weischedel. 1997. Nymble: a high-performance Learning Name-finder. *Proc. ANLP1997.* pp. 194-201. Washington, D.C.

Eugene Charniak and Mark Johnson. 2005. Coarse-to-Fine N-Best Parsing and MaxEnt Discriminative Reranking. *Proc. ACL2005.* pp. 173-180. Ann Arbor, USA

David Chiang. 2005. A Hierarchical Phrase-Based Model for Statistical Machine Translation. *Proc. ACL2005.* pp. 263-270. Ann Arbor, USA

Michael Collins. 2002. Ranking Algorithms for Named-Entity Extraction: Boosting and the Voted Perceptron. *Proc. ACL 2002.* pp. 489-496

Michael Collins and Nigel Duffy. 2002. New Ranking Algorithms for Parsing and Tagging: Kernels over Discrete Structures, and the Voted Perceptron. *Proc. ACL2002.* pp. 263-270. Philadelphia, USA

Michael Collins and Terry Koo. 2003. Discriminative Reranking for Natural Language Parsing. *Journal of Association for Computational Linguistics.* pp. 175-182.

Yoav Freund, Raj Iyer, Robert E. Schapire and Yoram Singer. 1998. An efficient boosting algorithm for combining preferences. *Machine Learning: Proceedings of the Fifteenth International Conference.* pp. 170-178

Ralph Grishman and Beth Sundheim. 1996. Message understanding conference - 6: A brief history. *Proc. COLING1996,.* pp. 466-471. Copenhagen.

James Henderson and Ivan Titov. 2005. Data-Defined Kernels for Parse Reranking Derived from Probabilistic Models. *Proc. ACL2005.* pp. 181-188. Ann Arbor, USA.

Heng Ji and Ralph Grishman. 2005. Improving Name Tagging by Reference Resolution and Relation Detection. *Proc. ACL2005.* pp. 411-418. Ann Arbor, USA.

Heng Ji and Ralph Grishman. 2006. Analysis and Repair of Name Tagger Errors. *Proc. ACL2006 (POSTER).* Sydney, Australia.

Thorsten Joachims. 1998. Making large-scale support vector machine learning practical. *Advances in Kernel Methods: Support Vector Machine.* MIT Press.

Taku Kudo, Jun Suzuki and Hideki Isozaki. 2005. Boosting-based Parse Reranking Derived from Probabilistic Models. *Proc. ACL2005.* pp. 189-196. Ann Arbor, USA.

John Platt, Nello Cristianini, and John Shawe-Taylor. 2000. Large margin dags for multiclass classification. *Advances in Neural Information Processing Systems 12.* pp. 547-553

Dan Roth and Wen-tau Yih. 2004. A Linear Programming Formulation for Global Inference in Natural Language Tasks. *Proc. CONLL2004.* pp. 1-8

Dan Roth and Wen-tau Yih. 2002. Probabilistic Reasoning for Entity & Relation Recognition. *Proc. COLING2002.* pp. 835-841

Cynthia Rudin. 2006. Ranking with a p-Norm Push. *Proc. Nineteenth Annual Conference on Computational Learning Theory (CoLT 2006)*, Pittsburgh, Pennsylvania.

Libin Shen and Aravind K. Joshi. 2003. An SVM Based Voting Algorithm with Application to Parse ReRanking. *Proc. HLT-NAACL 2003 workshop on Analysis of Geographic References.* pp. 9-16

Libin Shen and Aravind K. Joshi. 2004. Flexible Margin Selection for Reranking with Full Pairwise Samples. *Proc.IJCNLP2004.* pp. 446-455. Hainan Island, China.

Association for Computational Linguistics
209 N. Eighth Street
Stroudsburg, Pennsylvania 18360

Workshop on Annotating and Reasoning about Time and Events 2006

(ARTE)

Held in conjunction with COLING/ACL 2006

Sydney, Australia
23 July 2006

ISBN: 978-1-61738-505-6